Chapter One

When men ask how I got into this business, they always want to hear some fantasy filth about the sexual awakenings of my teenage self, probably involving words like rosebud, pert, smooth, curious. Girls, though, are always keen to believe that I've been sexually abused. I'm terribly sorry, but not knowing my audience this time, I'm going to have to bore and disappoint almost all of you. Much of being a good stripper, dominatrix, sex worker of any description, really - is saying and being what your audience wants. I can't do that here. I suppose I'll just have to tell you the truth or something.

Anyway, I'm not writing this for you, but for me, so take the truth and stick it if it doesn't confirm your prejudices or give you a boner. I want to understand, for my sake, how I got here. Because here is where I seem to be. I'm 36 now, and I can hardly go on pretending this is temporary; an extended summer job until my real life begins. I'm 36 and I've been doing this eighteen years, which is what, a third of my working life ? No, it's really happened. I'm a sex worker.

And it started the way most jobs do – or at least did in 1995 – I answered an ad in a local paper. It said :

'Dancers wanted! You will earn up to £600 a night. No experience necessary. '

That was it. Well, I liked dancing, I loved money, and I'd no experience of anything at all, so it seemed perfect. Certainly more interesting than all the admin clerks and care assistants and road crossing patrol attendants which were my other options. I rang up and was told to attend an audition. They held auditions every night at 5 p.m., turnover being so high, and men's appetite for new girls so insatiable. I was to attend the Windmill, just off Piccadilly Circus. My Mum was very impressed when I told her. She'd worked in variety herself, so the prospect of her only child jiggling for cash rather pleased her, not to mention the mention of the nightly £600. Now, I wasn't a total idiot. I was reasonably confident that earning £600 a night would involve more than a few high kicks on a sparkly stage. But – well – I just thought, why not ? I had just left Cambridge University, having gone rather mad after a year of abuse. (State school girls don't make it to Cambridge for a reason: they'd just hate it. It's a kindness, mark my words. Letting a girl from an Essex comp go to Oxbridge is like putting a pig into a Miss World contest – whether it's meant as a kindly gesture or a practical joke, it's not going to end well for the pig.) The point is, I felt I had nothing to lose. I didn't know who I was any more, or what I wanted. My whole life plan had gone to cock. What should I have done? The bald facts remained. I liked dancing, I liked money, I had little of either in my life and – so why the hell not ?

Ah, but it's a dangerous question, this 'Why the hell not'. It could have led me to far darker places than the Windmill. I was lucky. I wasn't a total idiot, but I was still, in all fairness, a bit of an idiot. So much so I turned up for my audition in leggings, jazz shoes and a leotard. I quickly realised my mistake when I saw the other girls, in heels, corsets and mini-skirts. But I was buggered if I was going to back out now, having spent all day working myself into a nervous frenzy about what I was getting myself into. Anyway, the other girls were sweethearts. We bonded. There were three students (from Goldsmiths - it really does seem extraordinary and disproportionate how many strippers hail from Goldsmiths), an Aussie backpacker, and a woman in her thirties who hoped to revive her florist shop with a cash injection.

We all talked for hours, waiting for the owner, Oscar, to return. He'd been delayed at court, apparently. We never did learn why he was there in the first place. It all seemed quite glamorous to my 19 year old self, rather than terrifying, as it might now. Honestly, I can't remember what we talked about, but I remember feeling happy, and accepted. No one judged you here. We were the dross, we had nowhere left to fall, nothing to prove. We were all money hungry, one and all, and prepared to sell our viewing rights to some of the flaps and folds we'd been born with, to fund our studies, our businesses, our children, our travel. We discussed them all, our needs and plans, and decided what we'd do with the money (£600 a night! £3600 a week! In 1995!) just as soon as the owner came back from court and saw us, and hired us on the spot.

We waited an hour. Oscar's son gave us a bottle of wine. We waited and talked some more. The florist talked about how hard it was running a business and looking after her kids now her fella had left her. The students talked about trying to keep themselves fed and housed in London on a student grant. The Aussie backpacker, a gorgeous girl with ginger corkscrew curls, had done it all before, all of it, and talked about how she saw each man as a walking, grinning giant dollar sign. She was the only one with any experience. The rest of us were clueless.

At 8pm Oscar showed up, charming, dark, glamorous, full of apologies. We were all pretty drunk by then, having sneaked a few extra bottles from behind the impressively stocked, charmingly unattended bar. We were told to walk out onto the stage from the wings, remove our tops, and then walk off again. This would, presumably, allow Oscar to gauge our capacity for embarrassment, and our stage presence, along with our tits. I loved walking out on that stage. I felt powerful, delirious with excitement, knowing all eyes were on me. But I also knew I hadn't a hope of being accepted, after struggling for some minutes with my leotard to produce a pair of rather pendulous, disappointing knockers. I went through with it, and watched excitedly as my friends bounced out of their sequinned corsets. I knew I hadn't got the job, knew it even before Oscar kindly instructed his secretary to take all our names and numbers, whilst surreptitiously pointing to the three he wanted. (Two students, one backpacker. Not the florist. I wonder whatever happened to her? Bet she didn't save the business. If only I'd met her today, I would tell her to take up domination immediately.)

I knew he didn't want me. I knew I'd wait in vain for a call that wouldn't come. And I knew, having had a taste of this life – wine, sequins, stages, girls with a cracking line in conversation and nothing at all to lose – that I wanted it all for myself. I knew it like I've never known anything before or since. This was where I belonged. I was a whore, down to the bone. I invested in some pretty underwear, hold ups, Ann Summers knickers, a lacy black dress from C&A that I actually still possess – just ask, and I'll show it to you some day. I went back the next night, in heels and a push-up bra, and wiggled my tits, nipples perked up with lip gloss, right in Oscar's face. Somehow I oozed confidence. Something about being on stage, having eyes upon me, made that happen. I can't explain it. But it was true then and remains so.

Somehow, I only felt I owned myself, my body, my space, when someone else was watching. It's not feminist, I admit it sounds a little creepy, but it still happens to be the bloody truth. So sit on it and swivel.

That time, I got the job.

~~~

I was selling vibrating hairbrushes at Waterloo station when I got the call. It was a simple job and I rather liked it, but now it was December it was decidedly cold standing on the concourse all day; plus, I seemed to have an unfailing knack for attracting nutters. My colleagues were charming, though – Tara worked with me on hairbrushes while Sam demonstrated snoods – and I'd told them all about my audition. They were just as excited as me when my phone rang.

"Hello ? " I fumbled desperately at my hairbrush, which made an astonishing noise, trying to find the off switch.

"Clara ? This is Ellen, the Windmill's housemother –"

"Ah, yes ?" I tried to sound nonchalant, and keep my phone out of sight of the boss, while waving frantically at passers-by with my hairbrush. Beside me, Tara saw my difficulty and tried to provide a distraction by shouting as loudly as possible "Luvverly hairbrushes! Cure baldness! Give massages! Make hair shine! Good for Christmas!"

"We'd like you to come in tonight for a trial run, and if you get along alright, look to taking you on permanently –"

Yesss! I did a little victory dance for Tara's benefit, which a passing lunatic promptly began to ape.

"Pop by at 8 or so and Sven will show you the ropes. Bring plenty of make-up and a couple of outfits – oh, and a garter belt –"

Resolutely I turned my back on the gathering crowd, trying to take in what I was being told. What was a garter belt again?

"Your shift finishes at 3.30 a.m., and we expect to see you here six nights a week. You'll pay £25 a night to work here."

Eh ? That was what I earned selling hairbrushes all day! And I'd have to be back at Waterloo at 7am to keep doing it. I could probably make it, as long as I didn't feel the need to sleep, ever.

"So, see you tonight. And Clara - what is your stage name? I'll need to write it down for the DJ ... "

Stage name ? Christ, of all the things I hadn't ever dreamt I'd have to worry about. I gazed thoughtfully at Tara, beaming encouragement at me even as she buzzed her brush enthusiastically over a bald scalp, and came to a snap decision.

"Clara – that's my stage name."

Pause. "Oh, right. I see. So what's your real name then, or would you rather not say ? "

Oh god, what ? Emerald, Crystal, Sprinkles, Gypsy ?

"Exactly, yes. I prefer to stay Clara – more … professional, you know ? "

"Right you are. See you tonight then. 'Clara'. "

I was pretty sure her inverted commas were ironic, but I didn't care. I'd got the bloody gig! Money, sequins, somewhere warm and alcoholic to spend my evenings! I did another little dance, and promptly sold more hairbrushes, purely on the back of my extraordinary enthusiasm.

Sam, on snoods, regarded me with the world weary cynicism of a mature 22 year old.

"You get sex job?" I nodded excitedly. He was Russian. That's a Russian accent I'm doing there. So was Tara. Although when asked, they both claimed to be Spanish.

"You never get away from sex job, once you start. You be sure you want this. I used to work door in brothel … " This was news ! "… so I know. Good money, yes, but frightening too. Police, drugs, dogs, guns. Valium for breakfast. Pretty girls broken up. You be careful now."

He turned away ponderously. Well, brothels sounded a long way from elegantly lit dancing clubs to my young ears. They were legal, for a start, and tightly regulated, swarming with bouncers. But I've often thought about Sam over the years, and how right he was. You never get away from sex job.

On her lunch break, Tara kindly fashioned me a makeshift garter belt from her laddered stocking. I slipped it into my bag, imagining it hung low with money. The money had started to take on life and shape in my imagination. I'd passed my driving test, but couldn't possibly afford a car. Pretty things, theatre tickets, treats for my Mum, just the sheer raw pleasure of seeing your bank balance without gasping in horror, all started to seem possible. The prospect of passing a shop window without automatically averting my eyes.

I sold thirteen hairbrushes that day, I remember, earning 65p profit on each. I gave token help with packing away the stall for the evening, but Tara shooed me off to the loo to get myself ready. I only had one dress, my audition dress. I'd stuffed it hopefully into my rucksack that morning, along with my heels, and the few bits of make-up I possessed. I popped into Boots for a sandwich and a shiny red lip gloss, the colour of old blood. I applied it in the station toilet, making faces at myself, giddy with excitement. It didn't seem real, none of it. I put on my dress. It was ridiculously short for street wear. If I leant forward even an inch I'd be showing my breakfast, but I had no idea if I'd be able to change when I got there, or if I'd be straight out on stage. I looked ridiculously young and skinny in my new garb, like a china doll, or a teenage runaway. Sam whistled when he saw me. "You look –" He hesitated, rolled the word round his mouth, lips twitching, then decided to say it – "Sexy."

I'd never been called that before! My innocence, as it happened, was my chief asset, my USP. Shame it couldn't last.

~~~~~

I attracted quite a number of lustful glances as I trotted over to Piccadilly, and lapped them up. This, I thought, was the beginning of a new life – womanhood, riches, admiration, adventure ! I sashayed into the club, pausing at the door to see if anyone was watching me. They weren't. Commuters bombed past, grey faced and hunched against the wind; a boy slipped into the phone box outside to post up the prostitutes' business cards. Well, well, I'd be noticed soon enough! I slipped inside, and hung about the empty reception for a bit, wondering what to do.

"New girl ? "

A plump, blonde woman called to me from the bottom of a well-obscured flight of stairs.

"Yes, um ... yes."

"The dressing rooms are down here, I'll show you."

She turned and began walking slowly, majestically down the darkened corridor, like a chubby Orpheus. Deep breath, chest out, I decided to follow her.

There were four dressing rooms in the club's bowels, and I was assigned to the third. This early in the evening they were devoid of girls ('100+, of all nationalities!!' the poster screamed), but they'd stamped their presence on the place – sequins and taffeta on the rails, feather boas on the coat hooks, the whiff of stale smoke, hairspray and perfume. It was airless, lined with mirrors and shelves, and the strip lighting was utterly unforgiving. I caught sight of myself and looked away hurriedly.

"Leave your stuff here, love. I'm Jackie, the house Mum. That's my room over there." She pointed to a little cubby-hole, stacked with boxes of make-up, sweets and glitter.

"If you want to use my stuff, you pay a pound."

"I ... brought some stuff to use ... "

"Righto. You might find you need more than usual, though. The stage lights wash you out a bit." She peered at my face critically. I backed away and she laughed. "Oh, you'll get used to that ! You better go and see Steve now. He'll need to check your hair."

I trotted away obediently, wondering if Steve was the club's on-site hairdresser, and whether I'd be able to save money on my usual dry trims if so. Maybe he'd do something exciting with my limp brown locks – curl them, pin them up with diamante grips?

The club looked much more impressive by night, all glittery, full of dark, seedy looking corners. The stage itself was spectacular, with a huge shiny pole whose purpose I couldn't even start to fathom, a hundred or so tables laid out around it, and at the back, a huge standing area around the bar from which the stage was barely visible. Later I learned that using these tables incurred a fantastic cover fee, which explained why they were generally empty till after midnight, when people were too drunk to care. A DJ's box stood beside the stage, where a man with a greying mullet was writing furiously. He saw me and waved.

"Hulloo! "

"Hello, um, do you know where Steve is ? " I shouted.

"Probably in his office" the man yelled back, unhelpfully. "Are you Clara? "

"Yes! "

"Well you can't be Clara, we've already got a Clara. Do you have another name ?"

"Er ..." My mind went blank. Again. You might think I'd have spent the intervening hours thinking up more suitably glamorous names, but apparently not. My middle name was Rosie, but I never admitted it to anybody.

"Most of the girls", he continued bellowing cheerfully, "use the name of their ex's new girlfriend ! "

Oh. Well, I didn't have an ex, just an on-off, love-struck idiot who would doubtless inconveniently kill himself if I ever left him, rather than shacking up with fresh lapdancer name material.

The DJ tutted. Then screeched:

"Tell you what, do you have a tattoo?"

"No!"

"Alright then, you can be 'Clara without the tattoo'. When you hear that you need to get on stage. Got it? "

I got it. And 'Clara *with* the tattoo', a short, sweet New Zealander with a giant scorpion on her left buttock, was kind enough to share her name. Sometimes, even now, I introduce myself as Clara Without the Tattoo at PTFA meetings.

I found Steve in the end, a dark, sallow man in a bow tie, a debonair Dracula who never smiled or slept.

"Clara? Welcome. Can you drop your knickers and lift your skirt?"

Ah well, here we go, I thought: this way to the white slave trade. I'd have to shag him to get the job, then I'd be trafficked into some Far Eastern brothel, when my cunt grew too loose for the Western market. Oh well, every job has its downside. I did as he asked. He frowned at my groin.

"You're a bit bushy. You need to trim up the sides a bit more."

He ran an experimental finger over my curls, and I gave a little shiver of fear, or excitement, or something. This is how it would be from now, I thought: constantly being judged and found wanting But only physically, which made a nice change from A-levels.

"Underwear's fine. Turn round, bend over."

For a minute, I wondered if he was going to finger my arse, like a prospective owner, and whether I'd let him, or if that would be my cue to walk out. But he didn't. I let the surge of righteous anger drain from me.

"Your bottom's a bit hairy too. You need to sort that out as soon as possible. But you'll do for tonight."

I pulled up my pants and turned to face him, still staring at me insolently.

"Novelty value, perhaps."

Sensing my interview was at an end, I drifted away and stood in a corner, feeling myself an awkward mass of limbs, without any idea of what to do with them. The other girls were starting to arrive now, bustling about, loud and important. They were a curious looking bunch, with no prevalent physical type. Fat and thin, young and old, blonde and brunette; I wondered how anyone ever got rejected. I suspect now it was confidence, charisma, stage presence that Oscar was after, rather than mere good looks.

A girl with long red hair and enormous tits was sitting at a table, and smiled up in my direction as she spotted me trying to blend in against the wall.

"Alright love ? New are yer ? Don't worry, you'll soon get used to it all. I'm Shona."

"Clara."

"Pleased to meet yer."

Her accent was broad Liverpudlian. As I watched, she began painting her nails with a metallic purple polish, whilst surreptitiously sneaking bites at a cream cheese bagel whenever the bar staff weren't watching.

"So … ", I swallowed, "How long have you been here ?"

"Four months. It's alright. Hard work, but you do earn. I'm buying my own house."

"Oooh!" I said, since it seemed to be required.

She nodded. "I'm doing a grand a week at least, so it shouldn't take long. Then I can go back home. How about you ?"

"Oh, I'm - a student. On a gap year." Which was true enough; I'd told my 'moral tutor' at Cambridge I'd be back in September, having taken a year away to become less insane and teary, a prospect he welcomed.

"So – what do I do ?"

She shrugged. "Just wander around and talk to them. You get £35 an hour for talking, £10 for a table dance – that's just down to underwear, you need to stay three feet away from them, they're dead strict – or £20 on stage for full nudity." Except she pronounced it "Nudd-ity".

"We used to get commission on champagne, but they've just stopped that. Shit, innit ? " as she saw my face fall. "But you're still expected to rack up a massive bar bill. Ask for champagne. If they won't stretch to that, go for wine. You'll still get plenty of drink, don't worry. And they won't keep you if you don't."

"And you still have to pay the £25 ?"

"Oh yeah. Don't worry about that, you'll make it easy. Just think of it as tax." She chortled at the thought. But I was worried. I didn't have £25 on me, or in the world, and the thought that I might end this peculiar night in debt as well as humiliated was simply horrifying.

"And what's it like, dancing on stage ? "

She shrugged. "S'alright. You get used to it quick enough. Don't even think about it after the first time. But you can watch me first, if you want. My regular's here."

A bashful young man had just slipped in the door, and instantly Shona's posture changed: in one smooth move she brushed away the crumbs, concealed her polish, stuck out her tits, and offered her most dazzling smile. I watched, entranced, as he bought her wine, and moved with her, arm in arm, down to the stage, where she slunk up the stairs and began to move. Not dance: there was no dance involved with Shona. She squatted down on her knees and moved back and forth. She licked her fingers and tweaked her nipples, and then seemed to slip her finger into her admirably neat front garden. She moaned and rocked in time to the music – roughly – while her young man watched, entranced. It was much ruder, and much stranger, than I could possibly have envisaged. Thank God she didn't go anywhere near that bloody pole. But I couldn't help but worry about the hygiene issues of stroking your fingers on that dusty stage, then sticking them inside yourself – never mind shaking hands with the fella afterwards, as Shona was now doing.

She grinned at me as she walked past, dragging her punter back to the bar, as if to say "See ? Piece of piss." Certainly it didn't look difficult. I had no doubt I could do something similar, should the opportunity present itself. I just hoped to God it would.

The place was starting to full up now, and I watched the other girls, dozens of them, glittery, stiff-haired, prowling and pouncing on the men with great shiny lipstick smiles. I gulped, checked my lipstick, and decided to make a start myself.

"Hello, I'm Clara", I announced, rather too loudly, to a fat, balding chap I thought looked! unthreatening, like a favourite uncle.

"Eh ? Sorry love. I'm only here for Jasmine. New, are you ? You'll be seeing a lot of me."

He gave a throaty laugh and slapped me affectionately on the shoulder. Definitely the affectionate uncle type, then, but sadly, not my uncle. I watched Jasmine sidle up to him, to be greeted by noisy kisses, a roll of notes, and a bottle of champagne. Arse. Well, maybe I'd have my own regular soon! I tried again. But while I met some charming men, I also got to hear some standard rejections. They'd just arrived. They were just having a look round. They wouldn't be staying long. Nice men, in silk ties and gold cufflinks, who spoke beautifully, through neat white teeth that had been nurtured by the finest dentists, and rejected me over and over again, with honeyed words and elegant smiles. I didn't know what to do. My feet ached in their unaccustomed heels, and my face hurt from smiling. I didn't have the right words, not yet. I wandered around the club, learning its geography, the pool rooms, the balconies, the quiet private booths. I drifted down to the dressing rooms to re-do my make-up. I gave myself a little pep talk in the mirror. The House mother was very sympathetic.

"It's just a numbers game, my lovely. The more you talk to, the likelier you are to get a hit."

I'd heard something similar from my vibrating hairbrush supervisor. I nodded earnestly, and redoubled my resolve. Plates of cheese sandwiches had appeared to help the girls mop up their champagne intake. I took three, determined to get me some champagne to justify them.

Bloated, but invigorated, I click-clicked back up the stairs, just in time to hear the DJ calling "Clara without the tattoo, on stage in two minutes please." Oh glory! And the club was teeming with bodies now, too: in my absence another hundred or so fellas had arrived, brand new quarry, moneyed, drunk – and expecting a show. I pulled on the arm of the nearest.

"That's me – I'm 'Clara without the tattoo'!"

"Oh yes?" he said, politely, a young chap, pink cheeks, eyes gleaming with excitement and beer.

"Well – er - good luck. I look forward to seeing what you can do."

"No, but, I mean, I've never done it before, it's my first time. I've never been ... naked ... in public."

"Really ? " Clearly he thought this was a line.

"Really! " Luckily the DJ cut in to confirm it.

"Clara without the tattoo', to the stage now please, for her debut performance here at the Windmill, or, indeed anywhere in the world ... Clara without the tattoo."

"Blimey! Well, gosh!" Bless him, he handed me his whiskey, which I gulped back with an attempted air of nonchalance, although in truth I nearly brought it straight back up.

"And how are you feeling?"

"Terrified", I said, immediately, and after a moment's thought, "Excited too, I think." More to myself than to him I added "I wish to God I hadn't had those sandwiches." But then the DJ saw me and started waving his arms in a manner I could only interpret as angry, so I had to leave this sweet boy man who suddenly seemed my best friend in the whole world, and take the long walk to the stage.

Now, I can dance. The dancing part, I thought, would be easy. It was just the logistics that worried me: how long before I started to disrobe, how much should I show, what if I couldn't manage to undo my bra ? Should I show each bit of me to each bit of the audience, like a magician will his deck of cards? How would I manage to retrieve all my clothes and leave the stage starkers whilst retaining an air of elegance and mystery, and reappear two minutes later to continue chatting to this boy man, whom I was now convinced would be my first hit ?

But my music had started. I had chosen Madonna's 'La Isla Bonita', since I knew it quite well and was reasonably confident it was short and snappy. I jogged on to the stage, heart pounding, and there gave my very best impression of a stripper. Like anyone else at their first day at work, I copied my colleagues as far as I could, faked confidence, and smiled broadly. And I absolutely loved it. I loved feeling the eyes on me, having the stage to myself, hearing the applause at the close. I seem to recall I gave a mock curtsey, found my clothes, and sashayed off stage, heart still hammering. It was more excitement than fear. And I wanted to do it again. I dressed as quickly as possible, and rushed back to boy man, but to my disgust he'd been completely colonised by another girl. But he did grin and give me a thumbs up.

Well, this was simply marvellous. I'd been here three hours, shown my tits to two hundred strangers, and I'd be paying £25 for the privilege. Fan-bloody-tastic. I felt new found confidence stiffening my spine. I walked back over to a table I'd already approached three times, where two men were talking earnestly. Perhaps, I thought, they'd like a little light relief from their philosophising. I decided to try a direct approach.

"Hello? Hello! Hello? Would you two like a table dance?"

They broke off to stare at me. One gestured that I should leave. The other one reached into his pocket, found a note and thrust it at me, then gestured that I should leave. I did as I was bid, then, by the light of the bar, unfolded the bill. It was a $100 bill.

A $100 bill! I had only the vaguest ideas what that would mean, in fiscal terms. But it was the first money I had earned for being naked, and precious for that reason alone. I was reasonably confident it would cover my £25 fee, anyhow, and maybe even bring me a little profit! Never mind that I had been paid to go away: it was money, and I was glad of it, and it brought me confidence to try for more. I was given a £10 table dance, then another, then another, and a couple of £20 stage dances too. I had an hour's conversation with a hotelier, who gave me £40 for my time. I walked out of there with £85 English money, and my $100 bill : I had 'done a one-er' as the cabbies say, and I'd had a bloody ball. I'd also drunk more than I was accustomed to. At 3.30 a.m. I was released from my stint, and staggered back to Waterloo station, where I'd be needed for work the next day. I didn't need sleep, or transport, or protection: I felt utterly invincible. And At least I'd know to wear my jeans next time.

~~~~~

At 6 a.m. I was woken just outside the loos by a tramp, who told me politely that my purse was sitting right on top of my open bag, and that anyone might steal it. I sat up from the metal bench where I had snatched an hour's sleep, smoothed my hair, and handed him a pound for his trouble. Then I checked my purse. All that lovely money was still there. It seemed extraordinary that you could have a night out, dance and drink and gossip, and come back with £100 more than you had before. It still does, really.

The shops were starting to open at Waterloo. I went to Boots for deodorant and toothpaste, and the currency exchange place with my $100. They gave me £64.38. Unbelievable! Free money! What a laugh, what a swizz, what larks !

Chapter Two

I stayed at the Windmill for four months, and during that time some of my greenness began to subside. I met rock stars, politicians, media moguls, and Michael Schumacher, whom I infuriated by asking what he did for a living ("I'm a very famous racing driver!"). I danced for soldiers and city boys, journalists and vintners. I was offered jobs, cars, jewellery, tit jobs and cash for sex, all of which I politely declined. I got a handful of regulars myself – a financial adviser, a chap who worked on the Daily Mail, a property entrepreneur. I didn't like any of them particularly, but they seemed oddly keen on me. Most of the punters infuriated me. I'm no good at sitting and talking for hours on end, but often that was the only way I could make money. I had to listen to them spew vitriol about their wives and bosses, but I didn't mind that, so much: most sickening, I found, was when they took an interest in me. I felt sullied by their enthusiasm for my youth, innocence, inexperience. So many of them wanted to cure me, to interpret my career choice as some sort of symptom, an erotically charged cry for help. Like Roger, the NLP expert.

It had been a dreadful night: all seventy girls out in force, perhaps twelve men between us, and only two hours before the rent was due. I had given up, and was doing a crossword with Alison, a girl I'd warmed to for being slightly younger and even less popular than me. She was skinny and angular with long black curls, like an ill-thought out boy, and she had a charming habit of offering fully nude dances for 'bus fare' even though bartering and undercutting the other girls was strictly forbidden. That night, she hadn't earned a bean, so I, from the relative comfort of my £40 from my Daily Mail fella, was thrilled to see a tall beardy man beckoning her over, pointing to a waiting glass of champagne.

"You're in there, my lovely", I said, cheerfully putting my feet up into the space she had vacated and getting back to my crossword. She sprang across the room, all curls and eagerness, and returned a minute later full of dejection, to shove the champagne under my nose.

"He – he just wanted me to bring you this. B – because you look so sad."

"Oh, for fuck's sake. What a raging scrotal sack of septicaemia", I said, while smiling politely and mouthing 'Thank you' in his direction. He smiled back and toasted me

"What does he think this is, an overstocked waitress convention ? Don't you worry, gorgeous, I'll go over there and screw some money out of that ill-mannered cuntwipe, and bring it back to you, OK?"

My language had deteriorated with impressive rapidity. Alison smiled.

"You don't have to do that …"

"Course I do." And I marched off to meet the fuckety fucking fucktard.

"Thank you so much", I beamed, extending a hand and moving in for a peck on the cheek, the only permitted physical contact. "My name's Clara. And you are?"

"Roger. I just couldn't bear to see how sad you looked. I thought I'd try to make you a little happier."

He spoke in squeaky, well-bred tones that had clearly cost thousands of pounds and centuries of in-breeding.

"Well, that's very sweet of you ! But I'm not sad, Roger, just a little bored, perhaps. There are so few men here and it's been ages, literally minutes, since I've had a chance to get my tits out, and they're starting to feel over-warm ..."

He shook his head at me. "Oh, there's no need for that with me ! You just don't want to be here, do you ? Tell me, where would you rather be? "

Well obviously I don't want to be *here*, you cretin, talking to you, I'd quite like to be in my bed, or sitting next to Alison working on twelve down, or even, at a push, talking to my Daily Mail man, who had an amusing line in tittle-tattle and a vicious tongue. But truth wouldn't get Alison her bus fare. Roger grabbed my chin rather painfully.

"I can make your dreams come true!"

Oh Lord. Spare me the mean, spare me the bored, but above all, spare me the lunatics. I'd landed myself with the holy trinity.

"Um ..."

"Nothing's too big if you know how to dream big ! "

"I'd like to be ..."

"Yes?"

"Richer? "

"Of course !" He gave my chin a congratulatory tweek. "Of course you would. Who wouldn't ? All you have to do is imagine it!"

"Oh. Really?"

"Imagine a nice big fat sum of money. Imagine opening your bank statement and seeing, ooh, tens of thousands of pounds written in black at the bottom! Imagine it! Now!"

"But surely a more practical step would involve your buying a table dance ..."

"Now!"

A small crowd was beginning to gather at his squealing, and I could feel Oscar's eyes on me. Oscar did not approve of scenes. I thought I'd better do as I was told. I shut my eyes for thirty seconds or so, smiled at the finish, then looked up to see him smiling encouragingly at me.

"See? Didn't that feel great?"

"Mmm. Ooh, I feel, oh, ever so inspired to go and earn a few a few more tenners right now..."

"You're thinking too small! " he shrieked, digging his fingernails back into my chin. "Do it ten more times!"

Oh Christ.

"Ten? Seriously? Wow, that's a lot. Ten? Right now?"

"If you're serious about accumulating wealth, yes."

He nodded, folded his arms and waited for me to begin. And Oscar crept closer, his piercing blue eyes on my face, lizard-like, unblinking, warning me to do as I was told. So I stood there, for ten minutes, faking concentrating hard, and adding a sudden flourish of excitement at the end. Ten times. A huge crowd of pissed up city boys turned up halfway through, so I could have been actually *making* money if I hadn't been stuck making a tit of myself next to this weirdo. Still, maybe the power of my positive thought had dragged them in ...

"Well, that was thrilling, thank you so much. There is a hostess fee of ..."

"Oh, you needn't pay me anything! The pleasure was all mine. Good luck Clara!"
And Roger bounded off into the night. Alison made her bus fare, and I made a few
extra quid myself. We walked down to the night bus stop together, and while
standing, shivering in the queue, both got covered in vomit emanating from the
drunk behind us. Explain that, Roger, I thought; for I certainly didn't dream it.
~~~~~
The rot started to set in at the end of January. The first few weeks after Christmas
we had a steady trickle of men, delighted to be free from the stifling, constant
presence of their wives and families. But by the end of the month the credit card
bills had started coming in, I guess. Certainly mine had. Suddenly the chief
difficulty of the night wasn't staying sober enough to find your bus stop, nor trying
to remember the name of the man with whom you'd spent several hours in intimate
conversation the night before. No, the problem was simply trying to get through
several dreary hours of nothingness. The girls started to bicker, out of boredom.
We weren't allowed books, reasonably enough. Nor were we allowed to sleep in
the dressing rooms. We had to stay in the club, watching and waiting, in case a
man appeared: although the sight of seventy girls staring up at him hungrily would
surely send most men screaming for the hills. Oscar let us all off paying our fees
most nights, in the knowledge that most of hadn't made it. Lots of girls left. Lots
more were fined for petty infractions of the rules. (Playing pool topless was
banned, for heaven's sake! Although it was a fun way to earn a few quid, and
actually I was getting quite good at pool). With my posh voice and girl next door
looks I was considered too risible to be worthy of firing. I clung on at the edges,
waiting for it to get better. I missed the money. How quickly it started to feel normal
flouncing home with a wallet crammed with tenners!
I'd been meeting a few idiots too. I'd probably been taking a slightly feistier
approach, out of desperation, and I'd met a few unpleasant, bolshy types in
consequence. I spent five hours talking to one chap, who refused to give me
anything when I refused to go home with him afterwards (and he was the most
ghastly, dull, arrogant wanker I've ever encountered in fifteen years of punters).
One drunken buffoon spat on me when I suggested a table dance. His spit dripped
down my dress, purple satin, formerly a favourite. I spat back, hitting his tie, and
he giggled like an imbecile.
But it was Valentines night that finished me off. I had assumed it would be bad, but
no-one came in at all until midnight. Finally, half a dozen city boys showed up,
drunk and braying, staggering into furniture while the girls circled them like
piranhas. I hung back, confident I wouldn't be their type, and anyway I had my
period and hated taking my knickers off, paranoid that the laserbeam lights would
show up the bits of blue sponge I'd shoved up my leaky gash. Anyway, one of the
girls was teaching me to knit.
One of them came bumbling over to me, fat, sweaty, a line of dribble drying on the
corner of his blubbery lips.
"Oi oi oi!"
"Oh, hello, how do you do?" I said frostily. My accent became ever more clipped in
proportion to the vileness of its recipient.
"That – bloke –" he said, trying and failing to steady himself on my shoulder, while
gesturing at the barman, " – said you had a hairy fanny."

"Oh yes?" I had no idea the bar staff ever looked at my genitals. They hid it well, but the place was dark, in fairness. And - I think I had done a drunken table dance on top of the actual bar the week before, unless that had been a dream. The barman threw me a sheepish grin whilst slamming a vodka and schnapps into a shaker.

"Have you … have you … got a hairy fanny? Minge? Cunt? Hairy cunt? Have you got a hairy cunt?"

He staggered into my face as he said it. I could smell him, sweat and money, and revulsion rose in me like nausea.

"Get off me" I said, and pushed him rather firmly in the face. He fell backwards and hit his head on a table. I think he may have lost consciousness for a minute or two. Then he lay there, giggling. A bouncer turned up and lugged him out of the club, while his mates bellowed abuse at me. I was a psychopath, a bitch, a cunt, a cock-tease. I'd had enough, I decided. If I wanted to suffer that kind of abuse I could have stayed at bloody Cambridge. There was some kind of row going on in the dressing room, so it was easy enough to slip on my jeans and coat, pick up my bag, and quietly walk out, keeping my £25 for myself. So out I went, and treated myself to dinner and a taxi.

~~~~~

I spent a week being unemployed. It was heavenly. I caught up with friends, moved from West Norwood to a fabulous vegan house share in Camberwell, a flock of geese in the back garden and a Buddha beaming at me from every room. A teacher and a care-home manager lived there already, and seemed curiously unmoved when I described myself as an unemployed dancer. I was confident I wouldn't be unemployed for long, anyway. I was nineteen, and more than happy to get my tits out, and during my four months at the Windmill I had found these were highly marketable assets.

Or I could, of course, get a proper job. I could work for that nice, independent wine seller, for instance. I considered it, I honestly did. But it all seemed a bit tricky, trying to make a good impression while leaving my tights on. I was still pondering what to do when I walked down Brewer Street one day to meet a friend for lunch. I was looking about me, as one might well do, at all the wonderful sights: the porn shops, the Raymond Revue Bar, handwritten signs and bits of cardboard telling of lingerie models. (You know, sometimes these girls really are lingerie models. That's the scam. A chap walks up a staircase expecting a shag, and finds a girl posing in a variety of knickers: if he suggests they take it further, a big beefy chap suddenly appears, explains the experience has already cost £100, and frog marches him to a cashpoint. But I digress).

And the peepshows, of course : 'Naked girls for £2' screamed the signs. Grumpy looking girls stood outside these places, presumably having been instructed to look enticing five hours earlier. Outside one stood a rather handsome man, who smiled when he saw me looking.

"Would you like a job?"

Never one to ignore the hand of fate, I smiled back.

"Yes please!"

"Dancing or Hostessing?"

"Dancing" I said firmly. I never wanted to speak to another heterosexual man again for as long as I lived, into which category this chap happily didn't fall.

"There's more money in Hostessing."

"Never mind."

"And you speak such good English too. What a waste. Well, we'll start you in the peep slots then. Wanna come see?"

I followed him into the tiny shop. To the customer it looked like a row of four sunbathing cubicles on a mucky carpet. Walk through the door marked 'Staff' however, and you'd find two girls sitting in their pants. One, who had a punter, was twirling round a pole. The other was reading Pride and Prejudice.

"So it's one girl to two slots? What if you get two fellas at once?"

"Just make sure you smile, and look at both of them. See, now –"

There was a sudden rattling, and another letterbox slot fell open in the cubicle of the girl already dancing. Two pairs of eyes were now following her cavortings. Without missing a beat, she draped her snatch over one slot, while pressing her tits against the other. In this position, her face was her own : she looked up and winked at me.

"Start tomorrow ? " the fella suggested. "Eleven till five, £40 a shift. If you're popular we'll get you some more shifts. Trial run, ok ? Bring a picnic!"

"And a book" muttered the less popular girl, sitting forlorn as her colleague sweated and pranced.

Well, I had nothing else to do, so I went along and found it was all good fun, really. It certainly cut down on all that irritating social interaction I'd found so debilitating at the Windmill. You sat in your cubicle, about the size of a disabled loo, separated from your co-worker by a pink curtain. In your workspace was a shelf and a pole. You could sit on the shelf and hide your bottle of wine beneath it, and use it to steady yourself on the pole when you had a customer.

Ostensibly, you were supposed to perform a strip show, but as £2 only bought the gentleman a minute of your time, there wasn't really much chance to piss about with boas and tassels. You could either sit about all day in your bra, or in your pants, so that you'd have just one garment to remove when a slot came down. I sat about in my bra. I've always been slightly self-conscious about my tits – they're not uniform shape or size, and I feel I need to tweak my nipples incessantly to get them looking pointy and perky. A minge is a minge, so I elected to keep that on show.

When a slot slammed down, you could only see a pair of eyes, and you could scarcely make out if you were being watched by someone young or old, or black or white. Not that it much mattered. You'd press your groin near their hole, and hear them wanking. Occasionally they would lift a finger to the slot and swivel it, indicating that they'd like you to turn round and show your arse. One chap, who turned up most days, would make a strange jingling noise as he tossed himself off, the result of several genital piercings and a handsome collection of signet rings, according to my boss, Mario. A rhythmic 'jingle, jingle, jingle' as I danced, like sleigh bells. When the other girl went to the loo, you could bet your bloody life all four slots would open at once, so you'd have to charge back and forth between them, pressing your crotch frantically against one window, then another, desperately trying to ensure that each customer got his £2 worth of minge.

I was fairly popular. I could tuck one leg behind my ear, and show them a split beaver all the way to my cervix, one presumes. I got given shifts three or four times a week, but I was still on the lookout for something more full time. After a steady grand a week, the money seemed utterly crap. And Mario kept scheduling my shifts to coincide with those of a German girl, who rather smelled, smoked incessantly and talked all day about how much she hated the Jews. To no avail did I sit pointedly reading the Guardian, or suggest that she move away from Golders Green: no, this was her sole conversational topic, how the Jews were taking over and conspiring against us. It quickly became wearing.

I decided to look more strenuously elsewhere for employment. But it was interesting while it lasted. I wonder if that beautiful German girl is still sitting there, day after day, cursing the Jews and showing her strangely rubbery flange, running outside every time her boyfriend rang to maintain the fiction that she worked in a clothes shop? I suppose not. Yet she seemed so much a part of the experience I can hardly imagine it without her.

Chapter Three

I don't want you to imagine I spent all my time wandering about Soho looking at brothels and their attendant businesses, and yet that was how I found my third job. I'd acquired a boyfriend who worked at Centrepoint, and he had a mania for vegan wholefood lunches – unusual in a man, and probably unique in a Scotsman. We'd go for mung bean salads at Mildred's on Wardour Street, and I'd try to decide whether I liked him or not, and if the mung beans somehow compensated for the huge quantity of beer he managed to swallow along with them.

On one of these occasions I chose to walk to the tube via Dean Street and saw the Sunset Strip theatre. It had three notices in the window ('New to Soho, Blue Pole Dancing!', 'Totally Nude Dancers' and, smaller and more prosaic, 'Girls Wanted'). I wandered in to enquire, and started what was to be two of the happiest years of my life.

The Sunset Strip was run by Freddie, an elderly, twinkly old man, white haired and dapper, who managed to be charming and respectful, while managing one of the most successful businesses in Soho. He saw me looking in, and gave a little wave from behind his desk, where he sat surrounded by pictures of semi-clad girls from the last five decades, all beaming stoically.

"Hello darling, can I help?"

"Well, I saw your notice in the window, about wanting girls-"

"Ah yes ? " He ran a glance over my figure. I was in jeans and a t-shirt, topped fetchingly with a fawn anorak.

"Would you like to audition now, dear? I'm sure we could squeeze you in somewhere –"

He ran a finger down a photocopied sheet, which read: '2.10 Juliet 2.20 Louise 2.30 Nina ...' and so on, all the way down to 9 p.m.

"You can take Juliet's dance in 10 minutes time, perhaps. She's been moaning about her knee all morning ... "

"Oh! Really? Now? But ..." – I looked down in panic at my jeans – "I haven't got any stuff. Clothes. And I've never danced for ten minutes before ..."

"You'll be fine, darling. It's only eight minutes really. We allow two minutes in between acts to reset the stage. And it's just wiggling. Just wiggle. The girls will sort you out." He reached forward and spoke into an old-fashioned intercom system.

"Girls! We've got an auditionee here. Can someone come and get her and kit here out for the 2.10 show ?"

A short pause, then a thick foreign accent crackled back to us.

"Freddie, is Nina. Coming now."

The moment she'd finished speaking, it seemed, a partially concealed door in the corner opened, and a tall, dark, clearly naked girl poked most of her torso round the corner, and winked at me.

"Hallo, Hallo! This way please ..."

Baffled by the sudden turn of events, I followed her down a murky little corridor, barely lit by a dim, solitary bulb. After the bright sunshine, it was like entering a dungeon.

"You dance before?"

"Ah, well, a bit. At the Windmill, you know?... just down the road?"

"Ah, Windmill are bastards. You were fired?"

"Well, no – " She looked disappointed, so I added "I just walked out! Ha! Owe them money and everything!"

If she was impressed by my latent criminal streak, she hid it well.

"You have clothes, music?"

"No, this is all a bit unexpected really –"

"Don't matter, you wear one of mine." And she opened another tiny door to reveal a dressing room, crammed to the rafters with girls, sequins, boas and smoke. It looked like the tiniest, most over-stuffed knick-knack shop in the world. Seven girls, in a room perhaps seven feet square, each with nine costume changes and a day's worth of paraphernalia – books, tuna salad, wine, shoes, phones, make-up. It was bedlam. They all looked up at me and murmured a greeting. I shuffled my feet and tried to avert my gaze. Walking into a room of mainly naked strangers never stops feeling odd. And now Nina was starting to remove my clothes and hold up an assortment of her own clothes against my shabby underwear, to decide which would do me most good.

"We must be quick, yes? You are on in five minutes."

"Oh, Christ, I –"

"Your bra is horrid. Best take it off. Knickers will do."

Fortunately, I'd put on a black lacy bikini pair this morning, boring, but passable. My mother isn't the type to warn me about always wearing clean, intact underwear in case of a car crash: otherwise she'd but fully entitled to gloat after this experience.

"This dress is good on you. You will wear this."

A tight, purple, clingy halterneck : it showed off my legs, and skimmed over my belly with surprising efficiency.

"What shoe size ? "

"Um, seven."

"Me too. You will wear these."

She kicked off her stilettos, and supported me as I pushed my own sweaty toes into them. I made a mental note to thank her when I was feeling less hysterical.

"You have a garter? " Another girl had popped up beside me, grabbing my arm as I wobbled. In truth, my shoe size is closer to eight than seven, and I'm hopeless at dancing in these towering heels anyway. Seeing my bewilderment, she lifted her skirt.

"You know, garter belt? For tips?" She twanged at a pretty white lace affair.

"Oh, no. I don't. Is that how it works?"

"Uh-huh." She pulled it off her leg and thrust it onto mine. I'd never been touched by so many people at once: it was like a porn film. Another girl was smoothing down my hair now, while another, possibly her twin, was brushing glitter into my décolletage.

"You like Prince?" Nina said encouragingly, as if to a simpleton. "May be Horny Pony?" She pronounced it as 'Hhherrrnee perny'.

"Um. Sure, why not?" At least being at the Windmill had taught me not to be precious about the music I used. Anything with a beat suited me. I could hear a muted ripple of applause from somewhere not too far away, followed by a rather louder squeaking.

"That's curtains" said Nina. "It is your turn. You are ready? We go down now. Here is Jessica". I heard a stomp, stomp, stomp up some stairs, interspersed with some heavy breathing and the occasional curse.

"Today is not so good for the tips. It is a good day to try out new things" said Nina, philosophically.

"But – but - what do I do?" I said in despair, as she started to lead me back out into the corridor, down some still murkier steps, covered treacherously in all manner of detritus.

"First song, take clothes off. Second song, dance about. Easy. Here is John. 'Horny Pony' John. See you soon. Good luck!" And she darted away, my newly found saviour, now truly totally naked, as I'd even taken the shoes from her feet. John was a sweet, elderly, dithering man who sat all day in a cupboard filled with thousands upon thousands of cassette tapes, all labelled in tiny handwriting. This, then, was the DJ. Not quite so flash as at the Windmill, but he gave me a friendly nod as he found the song and pointed me to the stage.

"You get a prop if you want. Bed or chair?"

"Chair" I said firmly. I'd some experience of incorporating a chair into my act: a bed sounded horrifying. He fetched it for me.

"There you are then. Off you go. "

And so, only ten minutes after I'd been walking along a sunny street with scarcely a care in the world, I found myself standing alone on a small stage, surrounded by thick red curtains, in an assortment of mismatched, ill-fitting clothes, listening to the coughs and mutterings of an audience I couldn't see, who'd paid money to be entertained: an entertainment I would now have to supply for eight, long, bloody minutes. The curtains began to squeak, and part. I arranged my face into something like a smile, and decided at the last minute to drape myself over the chair, Cabaret style, which won me a little bemused clapping on the reveal. I didn't dare look at my audience, not yet. Instead I began to run my hands over my body, in a mock wanky style that had served me quite well at the Windmill. I got more applause! There was actual mid-dance clapping for this nonsense, and a few cries of 'Jolly good!', and 'More!'. Encouraged, I took a peak. And saw a proper auditorium, though small, with about fifty or sixty red velvet chairs, half of them filled with men. Not Windmill men, these, but older men, quite a few pensioners, not a suit in sight. Although – what else could you expect on a Tuesday afternoon?

Still, it was depressing to see that a couple of them were asleep. I continued to wiggle. There were two poles here, right on the edge of the stage, so you could sweep your buttocks an inch from the audiences faces, if you fancied.

I had a little exploratory twirl. One of the more vocal men took this opportunity to grab at my thigh; I considered stabbing him in the face with my stiletto, but spotted the old man from upstairs standing at the back, watching me, and thought I'd best bide my time. God, how long was eight minutes anyway ? At least here there were three distinct bits of audience to dance to, whereas at the Windmill you either had some dots in the distance, or one man, who had probably seen enough of your tits and flange after a minute or so, but felt awkward about heading back to the bar.

The pensioners were still roaring their approval, and Gropey had another little go at my thigh. I felt that I couldn't really let this go unpunished, so I waggled my finger admonishingly at him. He blushed.

"I'm sorry, I couldn't help it ..." he murmured, and slumped back into his seat, crushed.

Wearing so few clothes made life tricky. I'd lost the dress and pants within thirty seconds, and found myself with another six minutes to fill with naked cavorting. Not knowing the songs, I had no idea how long I had been on for, and thought it impolite – nay, a deal breaker – to look at my watch. I decided to lie down on the floor, as my shoes were pinching. Huge round of applause. There can't be many jobs where giving up and lying down earns you an ovation.

Finally the noise stopped, the clapping reached a peak, and the curtain squeaked shut. Slowly, I rose to my feet, found Nina's now rather sweaty dress, and clambered heavily back up the stairs. I was out of shape. That would have to change.

The other girls were all hanging round in the corridor, looking rather sheepish, as if they'd all been peeping round the curtain at me, and only just got back in time. I handed Nina back her dress.

"Thank you so much!"

"Alright? How much did you get?"

"Get? Oh, nothing." That couldn't be good.

"What's this then?", said the tall blonde, flicking a finger under her garter belt. A little shower of pound coins fell out. That darling pensioner had been trying to tip me, not grope me! I picked them up. Four pound coins.

"Do I get to keep them?" I asked, in wonderment.

"Of course. £35 a day wages, plus all your tips."

It wasn't Windmill money, but it was a damn sight easier to come by, and the girls all looked so encouraging and pleased for me that I felt almost tearful. I climbed back into my jeans and went back upstairs to hear my fate. It would be too awful to go through all that, just to get rejected, with just my tube fare to show for it. I went out to see the old boy, pink faced and white haired, beaming at me like a jolly elf.

"Alright darling ? Could you start tomorrow?"

~~~~~

Chapter Four

The best thing about the Sunset Strip? It was almost like having a proper job. Five mornings a week I turned up at 10.45 a.m., and got let out to go home around 8 p.m. In the middle, I gave seven or eight shows, depending on how many girls were working, for which I earned £5 each: with tips, I earned a steady £70 to £80 a day, sometimes more. And when I wasn't dancing, my time was my own. I could put my clothes back on, go out on to Oxford Street for coffee, browse the shops, hit the pub; or, I could stay in that small, smoky dressing room and read my book. Freddie didn't give a damn what you did as long as you were on stage at the prescribed time. Every morning he would laboriously scrawl a timetable with our names in strict rotation from 11 a.m. till 8 p.m. hiding his handiwork whenever a punter came in. At twelve he'd finally finish it, calling through for one of us to collect it, hissing a warning if he saw a man glancing in its direction. He was an absolute darling, fiercely loyal and protective of us, and utterly dismissive of his clientele.

One afternoon a boy who who'd sat next to me in maths class five years ago recognised me from a poster outside, and tried to storm past reception to find me for a bit of a chat; Freddie knocked him sideways and sat on him, then calmly rang through to ask me to pop out to identify 'a certain gentleman' who claimed 'a prior knowledge' of me. Freddie also gave us £40 a week for drink, with which we bought value vodka and coca-cola from the local Somerfield. On hot summer days, we were sent to buy ice cream too, packets of magnums which he would dispense to us, twinkly and excited at our gratitude. It was like working for Father Christmas, apart from the pole-dancing and 'total' nudity.

And I found I quite enjoyed giving these shows. Eight minutes was long enough to give an interesting, creative performance, and I started to put some thought into my costumes and music. I was expected to have a few different outfits, so spent a few hours scouring charity shops for sequins, gauze, feathers. Encouraged to be different, to expand as a performer, I started dancing to the music I loved – Nina Simone, Billie Holiday, Dinah Washington – and quickly became known as the classy, serious one. I played on this theme, choosing outfits which were elegant and timeless, lots of long, dragging hems with slits up the side, sparkly shoes, hats.

I was so healthy and happy I was almost unbearable. I worked with a nice bunch of girls, the usual mix of students, travellers and mothers, not nearly so hardened as those at the Windmill: we weren't fighting each other for an income, so we could afford to be friends. Oh, the stories I heard! But these aren't my stories, and I can't repeat them – much. I remember a girl of gypsy origin, who had no idea of when her birthday was or how old she might be. A girl who'd trained at the Royal Ballet. A girl who'd performed at the weirdest of fetish clubs, could breathe fire from her snatch, and had to be discouraged from peeing on stage. The girl who claimed to be a 200 year old vampire, and used a bottle of fake blood a day on stage, covering tampons in it and claiming to use them as teabags: ('Keeps me young, dahlings…') There were prostitutes down on their luck, fired from their agencies and comparing notes, a Ph.D student writing a thesis on comparative religion; three Spanish sisters whom I never learnt to tell apart, and even one poor, pale soul who worked at the Sunset 11 a.m. till 8 p.m., then trotted off to the Windmill to work from 8.30 p.m. until 3.30 a.m. She slept in the corridor between her dances, and had to be woken and reminded to dance and eat.

It was all such fun! It sounds ridiculous, but it gave me routine and stability too, which my previous life had lacked. I dropped the pretence that I was going back to Cambridge to complete my degree, and stayed on for two and a half years. I might never have left, if only Freddie hadn't been bought out and dismissed.

Each morning I rose early and took two aerobics classes at the local gym, before taking the tube into Soho. Usually I had lunch with my bloke at some point, and the evenings were devoted to drinking. It was a very pleasant, mindless existence. Eventually I decided to go to Birkbeck to take a part-time English degree, feeling vaguely guilty that my brain must be atrophying. I read the books and wrote the essays sitting in my pants and heels, while around me half naked girls took drugs, had hysterics, worried about their children, debts, futures, sewed on sequins, checked their stocks and shares, or wrote their essays alongside me. It was chaos, but organised chaos, and it suited me. And all the time I learned more and more about the sex industry from all those wonderful girls' stories.

When I look back now, every day seems like it was perfect, golden, full of fun, like the way you're meant to remember your childhood as always sunny. There must have been some crappy days. I remember one girl showing up who was rumoured to steal, which led to a lot of unpleasant accusations and screaming, a dustpan and brush being thrown and a few bitch slaps. I went down the road for a pint, and when I came back, she'd gone. So that was fine. The Spanish sisters used to have awful, physical fights too, on occasion: I tried to intervene once, when one started to pour boiling water over another, but generally I left them to it. They could be gouging out each other's eyes one minute, and making up the next.

I started to get a few regulars, whom I could depend on for tips, and occasionally presents. Most weeks I would receive a bunch of flowers, four or five boxes of chocolates and some lousy poetry. A tramp used to lurk outside the Sunset at closing time, and we'd give most of the chocolate to him – we'd have become twenty stone, and toothless, if we hadn't. I kept some of the poetry, like this delightful offering:

You were so obviously new
The first time that I saw you
So gloriously young and fresh
That I,hopeful of a chance
To brush your luscious flesh
Proffered a perverted fiver
Your private dance to letch

So near, and yet so far
Your silky soft vagina
Fluttered before my eyes
As I sat mesmerised
By the ecstasy of your thighs

To boldly go
From Cambridge down to Soho
Armed only with your genitalia
So straddling the social high and low

Reveals your breadth of character

To get such satisfaction
In making so very happy
Lonely men like me,
Shows a warmth of vision
Which many cannot see

You became a stripper
To ease the Cambridge pressure
Now you have given so much pleasure
And voyeuristic relief
Give yourself, self-belief

You know there's more to you
Than your excellent essays on Rousseau,
Or men, with a mentality you eschew,
Viewing you, as just a screw,
You're unique, precious, only you.

I am sure, in the fullness of time,
You will find men wanting the beauty of your mind.
And with the arrival of real love,
Your confusion will come to cease
Relieved by the true satisfaction of peace.

One drizzly morning in June I turned up to work to find a little cluster of girls, miserable and idle, on the pavement outside. Usually we were all very keen to duck in as fast as possible, away from curious eyes, so this seemed extraordinary. I looked at Nina, who'd been there 10 years and usually took charge in a crisis.

"Has Freddy not shown up?"

"No, he here alright." She made a low gutteral growl of disgust deep in her throat. "Stupid bastard bloody bitch feminists glued up the locks. We can't get in. He's gone to borrow tools."
"Oh, shit."
"Yes. Exactly. Shit."
Around us Soho was starting to come to life. A few chaps I was pretty sure I recognised as punters were ducking past the Sunset and hurrying along to a club a few doors down instead, trying their best not to make eye contact with any of us.

"They left a note on the door saying 'Respect Women'", said Juliet. "But how is this respecting women exactly? People are staring and laughing at us. And how am I going to pay my childminder?"

There was a lot of nodding at this. The feminists didn't sign up many recruits that day. Freddy couldn't open the locks for us, so we all had to take the day off. The punters couldn't have cared less; they were surrounded by minge anyway. Freddie was rich enough to be quite pleased by the unexpected holiday. But the girls with children were screwed. Some didn't even have enough money to get the tube home. After a moment's hesitation, Freddie nipped off to the cashpoint so he could give us all a day's wages, rolling his eyes, embarrassed, at our gratitude. Juliet was ecstatic, crying on his chest. The rain cleared up, so I walked the eight miles back to my flat in North London, spending much of the time worrying about what I'd do when I was too old to strip. I was 21, and knew I couldn't go on beyond 30 without getting the piss ripped out of me by girls and punters alike. But still, I'd have my degree by then, and everyone knew what an economic powerhouse an English graduate could be.

At home I relished the pleasure of keeping my pants on all day, cleaned my skanky flat, and made vegetable lasagne and apple crumble, much to my boyfriend's astonishment, largely to piss off the feminists. Force me out of the workplace and into the kitchen, will you, you raging great bourgeois eejits?

On election day 1997 we made a banner for the stage, which read 'The Girls of the Sunset Strip support Tony Blair'. We wore red all day long, and danced to 'Things can only Get Better' until Freddie begged us to stop. Most of the girls weren't even registered to vote, but we all wanted to do our bit anyway. And we were all tipped handsomely by the crowd for combining political awareness with nudity. New Labour certainly seemed to promise a brighter future for the whores.

There were very few English girls at the Sunset. Most of the time it was just the ballerina and me. But our numbers were swelled one afternoon, doubled in fact, when a beautiful blonde arrived, grinning hugely, and very obviously pregnant.

Men love the pregnant girls. Jade earned 3 times as much as any of us, but she was too sweet for us to resent her, although we were all pretty glad she and bump would have to push off in a month or two. Her husband was in prison, so she was on her own for the next four years, and pretty much homeless, sleeping on a friend's sofa, and stretching their friendship to the limit. She'd saved enough money to rent a flat, but with no references, pay slips or bank account, and only a swollen belly to her name, no one was prepared to take a chance on her. She'd been to the council to get a flat, but was told she would only be housed by the time the baby was due if she were a battered wife. She told me all this one morning while I was applying my make up, then sat back and looked at me expectantly. I tutted with genuine sympathy, although half my mind was occupied with worrying about how best to remove my leopard print thong without the crusty bits showing. I was always too drunk at the end of the night to remember to take my pants home for a wash.

"So could you help me?"

"Eh? Oh, well, I'd love to, of course. But how?"
"Beat me up!"

"Oh, piss off. I'm not beating up a heavily pregnant woman. My karma's already shafted." I looked at her. "Why me, anyway?"

"Oh, I don't know...just because you're always so quiet I thought you might have a latent psychotic streak, I suppose..."

"Oh, cheers. No, that's just me being slightly shy, rather than plotting atrocities. You dope."

"Sorry."

"I should bloody well think so." She looked sorry, and utterly woebegone. "Look, do you want me to go round flats pretending to be you? I've got a bank account, no bun in my oven, and people tend to do as I say when they hear my accent."

She brightened. "Oh, would you? That'd be brilliant!"

In the end, though, she decided it would be easier to get beaten up, council rents being so much cheaper. I had to leave the room while it was happening, but a couple of the girls seemed awfully keen. Maybe they weren't feeling as magnanimous about all their tips disappearing as I'd assumed. They concentrated on her face and forearms, the bits that would show, and left her stomach in peace. She got two beautiful black eyes, and some fine bruising on her chin where they'd held her face still for the pummelling. She got her flat. Just in time, too: Freddy told her she couldn't work any more the week after, as she was turning his club into a freak show. She came back a fortnight after the birth though, and we all fussed over baby while she went on stage and earned a bloody fortune. Feminism in action.

Occasionally we'd get 'Modelling' talent scouts popping in, and soon I got my first modelling shoot, for Janus magazine. I played an aerobics instructor, wore a leotard and legwarmers, and took a very gentle spanking from a very eager old man, in a studio in Camden. It was brilliant fun, and I was really good at it. I found, after all that dancing, I knew exactly how to pose and show myself to best effect. I learnt how spanking photographers manage to time the click exactly to the impact of the hand on flesh, using a metronome, and exactly how to wrinkle up my forehead as though I was in pain. I did another shoot at a council flat in Streatham – toddling off by myself, like an idiot, to meet a man I didn't know, and take my knickers off for him. As usual, I was luckier than I deserved: he was utterly charming and full of good advice as to how I should pursue a career in porn, should I choose to. I didn't choose to, but it was interesting stuff nevertheless. And it was at the Sunset Strip that I met Finlaye. She burst in to the dressing room one morning, all blonde dreadlocks and bosom, bellowed "Alright then, smellies?" and sank down into the most comfortable chair, as though she'd already devoted a decade to the noble art of striptease, although in fact, this was her first audition. She was completely penniless, and had wandered in just on the off chance, having come down from Sheffield to London on the promise of a modelling job that hadn't transpired. The details of the modelling job, she breathlessly informed me over endless cups of sugary tea, were shouted at her from a moving car, just as she was off to the doctors to discuss the possibility of having her gargantuan, comedy, 34FF breasts reduced on the NHS. This mysterious talent scout, who operated from the back of a beat up Ford Fiesta, had mercifully persuaded her otherwise, and so her porn career was born. It's tricky to make a decent living from topless modelling, however, unless you are right at the top of the tree, and so she thought she might give stripping a whirl.

Everything that happened to Finlaye, it seemed, was just a delightful accident. I'd never met anyone so happy-go-lucky. She stayed in a hostel in Kings Cross most nights, except when she managed to pick someone up, when she'd 'Go home with them to save the £20'. She was noisy and outrageous, petite aside from her ludicrous great gazungas, and her seven inch nails, which were always beautifully decorated – she would spend hours painting them, covering them in glitter or studs, drawing minute snow-scapes or sunshine scenes, according to the season. I admired her tremendously. And my God, how she could drink! She made me look like an amateur. She never seemed to eat, but put away pints of lager from first light till the first encounter with her bed for the evening.

Quite often we would do double acts together, as she quickly got bored of spending eight minutes all on her own, without anyone to gossip with. She couldn't be bothered with all the sexy wiggling stuff, but went in for comedy strip routines instead, taking a newspaper from a chap on the left, and gravely distributing a sheet to every audience member. Then she'd take the glasses from everyone in the front few rows, jam them onto her knockers and stuff them down her pants, and then do a strange belly dancing routine, which ended with a big pile of spectacles on the stage. There must have been the strangest, most panicked scenes in the auditorium after we'd left: half-blind audience members trying to retrieve their eye-wear whilst obeying the cast iron law that they mustn't talk to, acknowledge, or make eye contact with any other member of the audience.

Eventually she moved in with me. She'd been hinting about it for ages, and had spent a couple of nights dossing on my floor when her lucky pants had let her down. I was living in Hendon, North west London with the boyfriend I still wasn't quite sure I liked. I saw very little of him, so I got very little opportunity to really make up my mind – he'd leave for work at 6 a.m., and I'd crawl home at about 1a.m. and try not to wake him with my drunken stumbling: on Sundays we'd wake together and both look baffled at the stranger by our side. Then he liked to go to Ikea to buy oddly shaped furniture called 'Smurf' and 'Froog', with no clearly defined place or purpose, which in any case he hadn't the ability to assemble. So I was rather pleased to have someone come to stay that I actually liked.

Theoretically, she was meant to pay rent, but in practice she was generally too skint, somehow, despite earning more than most at the Sunset. I didn't care. She was opening my eyes to a whole new way of being, and I loved her for it. Now my Sundays were spent having my nails blinged up, my hair bleached, my pubes and eyebrows ripped away, or shooting zombies on the Playstation she'd brought home one day after a windfall at work. She continued her modelling, too. One day she had to take a bus to a field somewhere deep in rural Essex, to sit topless on the back of a 'frozen' cow – literally frozen: there were patches of ice on its back – for a Milk Marketing Board calendar. I still have a photo from that shoot somewhere. She's grinning quite convincingly, despite the goosebumps, and the nipples sticking out like thimbles.

That Christmas we worked side by side on the Sunset Christmas show, a tradition in which a collection of large, white, styrofoam balls were placed on the stage for us to chuck at the audience, who then chucked them back. We wore red dresses and Santa hats, and cavorted to Christmas carols, while all the tips we received were divided fairly among all the participants, right down to the penny. Freddie doubled our drink money during December, so we were all of us pretty much drunk pretty much all of the time. Then the Sunset Strip closed for a week. Ross, the boyfriend, went to Scotland to see his parents; Finlaye went to Sheffield; I went home to Hertfordshire, rich, content, replete. When I came back to London on January 2nd, the Sunset Strip had changed hands, so that Finlaye and I were out of a job, and Ross had filled the flat with even more half-finished hunks of tat from Ikea. Arse and bugger. Bugger and arse.

~~~~~

January is a slack time for the sex trade, in general. Finlaye was better off than me, with her occasional modelling work, but I was well and truly unemployed and seemingly unemployable, at least for a couple of months. I was bored shitless. Fin and I used to go to auditions together occasionally, but they would usually want her and not me, which was dispiriting, particularly when she refused to take the job out of loyalty to me, which meant neither of us could pay the damn rent. Eventually she got a job at the Candy Bar, a lesbian pole-dancing club, which I absolutely insisted that she take since I (as her honorary girlfriend) would be allowed to sit at the bar drinking free of charge all night. She only lasted one night, though. Lesbians are surprisingly gropey, and one dug her nails into Finlaye's left breast until she drew blood. Shame – it was a good gig. Then we had a stint working at a rip-off dive of a hostess bar, with a handful of former dancers from the Sunset Strip.

We had to be there at 8pm, even though no one turned up until well after the pubs shut. It was too dark to read and too loud to talk, so we all just sat, glumly, staring at one another. No nudity necessary here: just cocktail frocks, smiles, and a willingness to tolerate and fleece drunken fools. After a couple of hours tedium the management set us to work peeling labels off bottles of cheap Cava, and replacing them with ones that said '1906 Krug', although you'd have to be pretty drunk not to see that they'd been run up on someone's computer.

Eventually two idiots walked in – tourists with very little English, so the headache inducing music levels didn't much matter – and picked Finlaye and India, one of the Spanish sisters, to go sit with them. They ordered two bottles of our newly doctored Cava, and half an hour later they were presented with a bill for £700. India didn't drink, so whenever her glass was filled she made a play of glugging it, then tipped it onto the floor when they weren't looking. It was enough to break my heart. Warm, sour Cava never looked so appetising. I spent the next four hours sculpting a little white reindeer out of the molten candle wax that had dripped on to our table.

Finlaye made £50 that night, Cava commission, but we didn't go back. When we left at 3 a.m. there was a noisy altercation between a bouncer and one of the tourists, who'd sobered up enough to realise he'd effectively been mugged. They were starting to shove each other when we ran off. A few weeks later, we heard a chap had been shot dead there. We didn't need it, we decided. With my fine grasp of English and her knockers we could definitely do better. And yet we didn't, for a couple more months. Finlaye started working at a hairdressers for a bit, to keep us in Playstation games and pizza. I found occasional work as a market researcher. My God, it was ghastly. All the effort and energy ordinary people had to exert, just to earn a few pounds! I admired them tremendously, really I did, but I wasn't going to keep them company.

Our luck turned when we'd just about given up, and it was my minge that saved us. Nina, the girl who'd helped me through my first audition, rang unexpectedly to say she was newly and gainfully employed finding girls for niche porn. She was traipsing round Eastern Europe trying to find girls who were unusually hairy, at least by western standards, when she remembered my peculiar resistance to shaving.

"Is very good job" she told me, with the energy and zeal of one who worked largely on commission.

"Lots of work, magazine, film, website, all you want. Webcam use you once a week at least. You make good living easy."

It couldn't be worse than market research, anyway. She gave me the number.

"Tell Sean that Nina sent you!"

Finlaye spent her last quid on a celebratory bottle of cider, convinced my muff would be an end to all our woes. With her newly acquired hairdressing wiles, she insisted on shampooing and conditioning my groin warmer, bouffing it up with mousse and spray, and talking admiringly about my crop, our harvest, that would see us through the winter. She even started growing her own, but mine had taken years to achieve, and her own thin, wispy, blonde little strands didn't promise anything too spectacular anyway. Instead she concentrated her efforts on my neglected appearance, helping me choose an outfit, and doing my make-up and hair, both ends.

Sean had an office in Golders Green, stocked with bright lights and cheap wine. He was a lean, gangly man, deadly professional, completely uninterested in my young self except as a tool to earn him money, which is always reassuring. Girls, you really needn't worry you'll be molested and harassed by porn barons and pimps if you get into the sex trade. All the ones I've ever met are either gay, or sick to death of flange. You're just a product to them, nothing else.

"Clara? In here, please darling. Could you drop your pants?"

And I did. In fact, I nearly dropped my pants at the market research interview: I'd never been for a job where it wasn't their first question. Sean ran his fingers through my pelt, as if he were considering buying a rug.

"Mmm-hmm. Not bad. How long have you growing this?" He made it sound like a career choice, rather than laziness and a propensity to shaving rash.

"Um – ten years or so."

"Do you shave anywhere?"

"Just a bit, here, on the inner thigh."

"Well, stop it."

I kissed goodbye to swimming pools and bikinis.

"Fair enough."

"I'm sure I can get you some work. Mainly Yank stuff. They're nuts for it. It's the new taboo. And webcam work. Done webcam before?"

" It's easy. Can you read?"

I assured him I could.

"You'll be fine then. Read what the punters say to you, respond, type something flirty back if you like. Two hour sessions, £200 a time, ok?"

"God, yes!" He grinned at me then.

"I'll set you up with some photographic work too. You'll be fine. And if you see any other hairy girls, pass 'em my way, won't you?"

He turned back to his computer, where he was photoshopping a little extra bush onto a pair of dusky thighs, and I assumed I had been dismissed.

The next day I got a phone call inviting me to a webcam studio, the location of which was a mysteriously well-kept secret. I was instructed to 'come alone ... and wear something dowdy.' It was in a pretty rural part of England I'd never heard of, an awfully long way to travel when you're skint: Finlaye had to pawn one of her many engagement rings to raise the train fare. Even now, fourteen years later, I'm nervous about mentioning the exact location in case I wake up next to a horse's head. They were just that type.

A slight, dark middle-aged man with a limp and a shy smile opened the door to me, in an industrial unit in the middle of nowhere , and quickly ushered me inside.

"Find the place ok? You didn't ask for directions, did you? No one saw you walk up?"

"Jesus. I don't think so ..."

"The landlord thinks that we manufacture precision scientific implements. We got run out of Dagenham last year. We simply can't be too careful. In here, in here – "

He showed me through a cluttered corridor and into a tiny room decked ceiling to floor with monitors. On most of them a skinny girl lay on a bed with her legs spread, pubes glistening proudly, clearly well oiled, with a gigantic dildo stuffed up her. Occasionally she would get up from this uncomfortable looking position to glance at the computer screen before her, smile, and change her position, or do something new, tweak her nipples, show her arse crack. It looked simplicity itself.

"That's Anna. Russian girl. Her English isn't up to much, but she can more or less understand what they are typing to her. See?"

He pointed to a screen filled with text. Sure enough, it showed a line of men's names, followed by instructions: Anna, show us your pink, shove that green dildo in harder, I love your pretty pert tits, will you go out with me, where do you live, I dream about you all day long, and on, and on. It was like a collective male psyche, unfiltered, unedited and rather badly spelt.

"Ideally she'd be writing back to them too, but it's just beyond her grasp of English. But we'd like you to type and strip, if you would."

He looked at me for the first time.

"You'd better get changed and get your slap on doll, you're on in five. The loo's through there."

He pointed to a grubby little cupboard.

"I'll give you a big build up. Don't let me down."

Not being quite certain what my job involved, I wasn't sure how I could let him down, but I nodded and promised fervently that I would Do My Best, and tried to look earnest as I said it. Then I nipped into the loo, where Anna had already taken up most of the available space with a frightening collection of uniforms and props. I'd only brought one dress and a pair of heels. I put them on, feeling rather pathetic and uncertain. Anna had even surrounded the basin with a variety of perfumes. Maybe she needed to smell like a tart to get into character. I picked up one and sniffed it, then smashed it back down guiltily as I heard her approach. She stormed in naked, threw a pile of clothes into the corner, and yelled 'Fucking Bastards!!' in my general direction, then began to brush her hair out furiously, as if it had caused her offence. I made what I hoped were suitably sympathetic noises and scuttled away back to the room of computers, hoping to God I passed muster.

The man with the moustache barely glanced at me, so fascinated was he by his own praise.
"There you go doll, cop a load of that!" So cop I did :
'A real treat for you today, a beautiful, sexy lap dancer, never seen before on the World Wide Web! Brunette, green eyes, nice neat tits and a bush to die for!! Gentlemen, start your engines!!!'
He looked up at me proudly.
"Good eh ?"
"Very. I just hope I can live up to the notice."
"Acch, you'll be fine. Piece of piss. Come on, I'll show you round the studio. Don't worry, the camera's off."
I tip-toed after him. I was feeling horribly nervous. I'm not a natural beauty, far from it. When stripping, I'd developed a knack for letting my personality shine through, interacting with the punters, wearing an expression which I hope conveyed 'Obviously this is ridiculous, that you're sitting down there while I wiggle about up here showing you the bits I was born with, but let's just make the best of it, shall we?' I hated the idea of not being able to see or manipulate my audience, of just being judged on my appearance.
"Here are your dildos, which are sterilised every night."
I categorically did not believe that.
"More batteries, if you need them. Nipple clamps, paddles, all that sort of thing, are over here."
Was I meant to torture myself as well ?
"And here's the keyboard. You can see yourself up here on that monitor, and you can see what they're typing here."

They were already typing, wondering among themselves what the new girl would be like, if she'd be as awful as Sally or as fat as Pam. It did nothing to assuage my fears.
"The cameras are here, here and here. When they're on, you have to assume some one can see your every move. No picking your nose, or reading a book. You're on stage for the whole two hours. Got it?"
"Got it. I think. And – but –" as he went to turn on the cameras, panic rose in me " – What exactly do I do ?"
"Whatever they tell you to do, of course. Within reason."

He paused to consider.

"And I wouldn't penetrate yourself with the bed post if I were you. Anna has already done that today, and I'm not sure she's totally clean ..."

I looked at the bed post, which was the size of a sturdy bollard, and assured him I wouldn't. He crept out of the room. I sat on the bed and looked at the screens. A terrified looking girl, pale and exhausted, stared back at me. I sat up straight and tried a cheeky wink. Not so bad after all. The light was wonderfully flattering. The other screen, filled with text, started scurrying past my eyes like ticker tape.

- Hello
- Hello new girl
- Are you really new ?
- What's your name then
- Take your knickers off
- Have you got a boyfriend

A disembodied voice suddenly boomed into the room.

"Darling, I meant to say, get your tits out by 2.30, your bush by 3 and stay naked for the final hour, ok?"

I nodded.

"Don't nod! They can see you, remember? Type something back to 'em!"

I looked down at the worryingly oily keyboard, and wondered what to type first. All those conflicting demands kept coming.

- Show us how wide you can spread your legs
- How many fingers can you get in?
- Do you make a lot of noise when you cum?
- Do you know Destiny she's a lap dancer too?
- Can you give me your number. I'm an amateur photographer, you can trust me.

I took a deep breath and started typing. Typing I could do.

- Hello every one. My name's Clara. I'm new here, and new to webcam, but I've been in the sex industry for three years and I'm not an idiot.
- Who'd like to explain to me what happens next ? The politest answer gets to choose my first pose.

And we were away. They seemed genuinely delighted I could write back to them. Some of them were quite good fun, and we got on famously. The two hours whizzed past. I had to be reminded to take off my clothes and make with the sexy. I picked up a dildo and sniffed at it dubiously. This resulted in a banging on the wall. I tried to pass it off into a sexy licking motion. Actually, it did taste slightly of disinfectant. I was probably safe after all.

The job consisted entirely of lying on a bed and occasionally sitting up to type bollocks, both occupations at which I excelled. I learnt how everyone started going quiet, or making ridiculous typos, the ruder I became – the trials of typing left handed, presumably. Moustache man seemed pretty pleased with me, muttering about click rates and viewing figures, and promising me a regular slot each week. Perched on top of my bag I found an envelope with 'Hirsute: £200' scribbled on it. Inside were ten limp notes. Salvation.

~~~~~

I did a few hairy porn shoots, stills and film, after that, all ludicrously well paid and – well, just ludicrous. Modelling was dull and physically demanding – they were determined to get their money's worth out of their models, so I would usually spend twelve hours or so in the most extraordinary positions, legs behind my head, doing shoulder stands in the bath, leaning backwards out of windows, legs splayed, all to show off my genitals in a new and unusual way. Luckily I was pretty flexible. I developed an ability to go off into a zen-like trance state, and would come to, to find a young man crouched between my thighs, brow furrowed, camera the size of an elephants head flashing away at my lady parts. The Americans liked to learn something about the models too, so at the end of each shoot I would be presented with a four page questionnaire, asking me the most baffling questions. What was my favourite pudding ? How old was I when I was first kissed ? Who was my most embarrassing celebrity crush ? What was my position on capital punishment ? God knows what the Russian girls made of it. I answered diligently, but not having ever seen any of these magazines, I've no idea how much they used. Probably a single speech bubble, like the page three girls. 'Clara, 23, stopped pruning her bush twelve years ago, and thinks universal nuclear disarmament is something we should all strive towards!'

Finlaye discovered she was pregnant around this time. She hid it as long as she could, with corsets and fanciful stories about trapped wind and beer bellies, but at seven months she was chucked out of her lap dancing job. God knows why : she was earning an bloody fortune. Men love the pregnant girls, as long as they're not married to them. She did a little 'Poppin Mama' porn after that, but found it too perverted even for her taste, and decided to go back home to her parents in Sheffield. I missed her dreadfully. When the baby arrived, its head was quite flat on one side, 'from all the corsets' Finlaye claimed. Now I'm Facebook friends with that baby. Extraordinary.
I decided to chuck my on-off boyfriend, largely because I wanted a baby too, and he emphatically did not. I had accumulated a decent amount of money, and bought myself a pretty cottage in the suburbs. The neighbours were politely suspicious of my youth and independence. I started a rumour that I had inherited most of my wealth and did a little freelance tuition for the rest, which hurt my pride horribly, given I'd spread my legs for every sodding brick. But you can't go shouting that sort of thing in Hertfordshire. So there I was, twenty three, with a pretty house, a ridiculously well paid career, and a hankering to become a mother. It seemed the next logical step in my ludicrous existence. What was the point of all this material wealth if I had no one to share it with and bequeath it to? I decided to find a man. I thought it couldn't be too difficult. After all, I met hundreds of the things every day, walking sperm tubes, all generally babbling about their keenness to fill me with baby porridge. I started worling the London pub strip circuit, accumulating so much cash it became a fire hazard, but always with my eye out for a suitable partner.

When I started, there were over seventy pubs in London which offered nude dance along with your pint. Most have closed down now, or put a stop to the nudity. A combination of over-zealous regulations from Westminster City Council, and the general decline of public houses, topped off with the smoking ban, means it's nearly impossible to earn a living doing the circuit now. In 1999, though, they were at their peak, and the ugliest idiot could have made their fortune within a couple of years.

This is how the pubs worked. An agency had a couple of hundred girls on its books. Most pubs had a lunchtime and an evening shift, usually requiring two or three girls for each shift. So we were all kept busy pretty much all day, every day. The pubs paid the agent. The chaps didn't pay an entrance fee: instead they'd put a fifty pence piece or a pound coin into our glass as we walked round before our dance. It was wonderfully exciting. We'd do a three minute dance, and earn perhaps £150 for it on a busy night. Then put our clothes back on, pick up our glasses, and troll back round again, over and over. It was silly money, dirty money, smelling of beer and fags, sticky with sweat and aftershave. How my back would ache of a night, lugging it all back home. God knows what the bank made of me, turning up each morning with sackfuls of change. Probably that I was one of those super-successful beggars so beloved of the Daily Mail. Not so far off the mark, actually. Each morning I'd take the train into London, my cheap, battered old hold-all stuffed full of sequins, boas, crusty old knickers, CDs and sandwiches, and every night come back quite drunk and weighed down with money. It's a wonder I was never mugged, chinking steadily as I wove my way along. But I suspect the neighbours may have started to suspect I wasn't the quiet heiress and private tutor I claimed to be.

I tried, periodically, to get pregnant, but the men I met were generally such louts I could only bear to spend a single evening of their company. I was living such an unhealthy lifestyle, it was probably very lucky that I didn't succeed. I didn't try to deceive men. I'd see a relatively handsome one, shove my pint glass under his nose and say : 'Would you like to contribute to my dance, please ? ' and once he'd obliged, 'and would you like to make me pregnant too ? ' It was amazing how often that worked. I'd explain I required no financial or emotional support, just a few drops of that stuff I seemed to elicit so naturally anyway.

The agency was arranged alphabetically, so I generally found myself working with Chrissie, Christina, Claire, Clarissa and Courtney, without any idea what Annabel or Zenka, about whom I'd heard so much, (none of it complimentary), might be like. Of my co-initialled colleagues, I liked Chrissie best. She was posh, plump and absurdly over qualified, writing a PhD on Medieval Popes, of all things, and forever suffering marital trouble, of which I heard more than I would have chosen.

There were a lot of quiet afternoons spent sitting in bars in Shoreditch, buying each other pint after pint, and discovering her partner's peculiarities. Josh was the jealous type. Why would a jealous type marry a stripper ? Beats me. Maybe he liked the drama. Every half hour she had to ring him to explain how bored she was, how utterly un-turned-on. It was nearly impossible to get into a rhythm with any punters with that nonsense carrying on.

"He found a stain on my skirt" she confided in me, as we sat gobbling chips one rainy Monday lunchtime, waiting in vain for the bankers to stop banking and pop in for a perv and a pint.

"He was absolutely convinced it was spunk. But it was mayonnaise ! He thinks I'm having an affair with a bloody jar of Helman's ! "

I tutted sympathetically and tried to avoid looking at my watch. Slow days were a killer. I was sure I could feel my face wrinkling, my ovaries withering. Chrissie hid her chips under her frock as the landlord walked past.

"I'm giving this lark up," she went on, poking suspiciously at a pube on her chip box. I'd heard that before, almost daily, and told her so.

"No, really. I mean it. I'm getting a job where he just can't be suspicious of me, somewhere – "

A crèche ? A nunnery ?

"Somewhere where the money is so quick I just wouldn't have time to do anything else. He just won't believe that I can spend ten hours in the pub, and come home with £30 … "

Had he not seen her drink ?

"I'm thinking about strippergrams. Fancy it?"

"Um … "

"My mate Michelle runs this agency, and they're always looking for girls. The joy of the strippergram is, whatever the hell it is you're walking in to, you know it'll all be over in five minutes. And they've booked you, they want you, and you know you're gonna make someone's night. Beats sitting around here all day, waiting for someone to notice you, no?"

"Hmmm … I dunno..."

"There'd be no talking to 'em, no hanging about. You get four or five a night, and that's an easy £200, and the whole day to yourself too."

It did sound extraordinarily attractive. I could spend all my days meditating, drinking smoothies and painting the nursery, rather than hanging out in bloody smoky bars. Chrissie pushed a business card at me.

"Go on, give her a call."

I did, the next day. The decision was rather made for me when a banker finally showed up at the bar, picked me to do lap dance after lap dance in the roped off area in the corner, demanded to see my bottom at closer and closer quarters, my bottom cheeks spread as wide as I could make 'em, pressed almost onto his nose – until finally the inevitable happened, and I farted in his face. He was appalled, and shouted about it rather noisily. As if his particular predilections were my fault.

I spoke to Michelle, an elderly sounding woman with a thick Essex accent. I gave her my by now immense CV of relevant experience, she sounded suitable impressed, and explained the job to me. It sounded easy enough and indeed, wonderfully quick. I promised to start looking into obtaining some police woman and traffic warden uniforms, and to call her when I was ready to begin. Ten minutes later she rang me back.

"Actually, could you do one this lunchtime?"

"Oh God, really?"

"Yeah, it's meant to be me, but I really can't be bothered."

She stripped … this woman who sounded like my Granny ?

"It's a 40th birthday, at the Harvester in Harrow."

A Harvester, on a Sunday lunch time ? Was that even allowed ? Surely it would be swarming with kids?

"Ach, it's only a topless. You're meant to be a police woman, claiming he's parked illegally, but you can just say you're plain-clothed!"

She cackled heartily at this. Turned out it was one of her favourite jokes.

"The victim's name is Steve. The contact is Dave. He'll meet you outside the pub at 1.30, with cash, £60, of which I get £20. Got it?"
I got it. A baptism of fire. 'In and out in five minutes', I kept telling myself on the drive. I knew that pub. I had eaten there with my Mum. It seemed just extraordinary to be marching in there now and getting my knockers out. Just imagine it, ambling into one of your favourite pubs and stuffing some secondary sex organs into the face of a stranger, probably while he was eating his roast and his kids were running round his ankles, hyped up on cola. Imagine that. You'd probably refuse, wouldn't you? Shake your head in wonder that anyone could ask something so ludicrous of you? So why the hell didn't I?
I cobbled together a rubbish police outfit, consisting of short, tight black skirt, white blouse, hold-ups and high heels, and a silky black scarf knotted vaguely round my neck. It didn't matter a bit though, as they were all expecting me, and insisted rather noisily that I remove my clothes as soon as I walked in. I closed my eyes, and did as I was told. Heaven knows what time they'd all started drinking, but most of them could barely stand. I had to chase my victim round the dinner table, in true Benny Hill style, and eventually half sit on him while I removed my clothes. Handcuffs, I thought: next time I'll bring handcuffs. And a truncheon. The boys all called for the victim to be given a birthday spanking, which I gladly gave, and seemed to think that my tits should be covered in whipped cream and wobbled in his face. I explained that I'd only been in the job less than an hour, and hadn't had time to pick any up. A leftover bowl of ice cream was procured from a nearby table, and substituted, to reasonable effect. It was a bloody sticky business, though. I popped into the ladies for a quick wash down, but the scowls and glares I received there soon sent me scuttling away again. Another note to self: next time, bring wet wipes.

Girls, know this: taking your clothes off in front of men makes them happy and mellow, but repeat the trick in front of girls and the girls get very cross indeed. Also: men aren't the least bit fussy. With very few, probably gay, exceptions, men don't notice saggy tits, pot bellies or a touch of cellulite. They're just so pleased that you're naked, the rest are a blur to them. Girls, however, won't rest easy until you've been pulled to pieces. Over the delicious sound of chaps panting, I could still make out a low undercurrent of female mutter: look at the size of her arse! I could do better than that! And why the hell doesn't she trim that minge?
Such dreadful insecurity among women is, of course, a tragedy and a blight, and I would really like to have told all these girls the secret: men really don't care how you look, so it's pointless being jealous of me. But if I'd got any closer, they'd probably have glassed me.

Michelle must have got a good report back, because I got the job. Strippergrams tended to happen back to back on a Friday and Saturday night, so I had the rest of the week for myself for webcam and porn, and the odd well paid pub shift. The most money, by far, though, was from those weekend strippergrams. I very much enjoyed the work, aside from all the endless driving and getting lost. I got to know Herts, Essex and North and East London so well I could probably have turned cabbie, if I'd fancied. I found myself a police helmet and a naughty nurses outfit, and was rarely asked for anything else. The nurse thing was quite often requested at residential homes, to celebrate patients ninetieth or hundredth birthdays – always nerve-wracking grinding away on a centurion's lap! Occasionally I was asked to turn up as a Nun, and I would improvise with a black sheet and a crucifix ; once I was asked to dress as a 'grungy art student' for the opening night of some surreal play – I turned up at the after-show party and manage to snaffle a fair few canapés before I found the director, and took off my luminous tutu and stripy leotard, to thunderous applause.

The worse type of gig was generally in an office. Horrid fluorescent lighting, no atmosphere, Tuesday 11 a.m. and me trying to get through security to see Mark in accounts, who was fifty yesterday, and is still nursing a banging hangover. Most of my gigs were in pubs, with music, booze and chatter as a backdrop, and I hardly ever remembered to bring a stereo with me. The three minutes I spent disrobing to total, stunned silence, twenty two office workers staring at me joylessly, the women scowling, the men shocked and nervous at their own arousal, must have been the longest of my life. Even if I remembered a CD player, in those huge, echoey offices its tinny, trilling pop beats seemed to make the whole experience even more pathetic. Still, at least I tried.

I was sent to do a job at a warehouse in Herts, which stocked huge quantities of designer creams and make-up, and came away laden with free samples - what a coup! And I had to do a few in the open air, on building sites, with special protective boots, helmet and fluorescent jacket, and nothing beneath – they were always a giggle. No girls present, and lots of exciting pieces of equipment for me to improvise on.

My stash of coins began to be enhanced and buffeted by bundles of notes. I kept my cash in a Quality Street tin, and took real, nerdy pleasure in watching it grow, week by week. Strippergrams were useless for finding baby-fathers though. If their chief advantage was their speed, it was also their disadvantage. I must have done thousands of the things, shown my gash to tens of thousands of people, but now there are very few I can remember, and those mostly because they were unpleasant. But I enjoyed the job, in the main: it was fun making people's evenings enjoyable, particularly the stag parties, who always looked bored shitless when I turned up, as if they knew they ought to be doing something decadent and crazy, but just couldn't think of anything. I knew just how to handle them. Blindfold, handcuffs, paddle, whipped cream, ice cubes. Lovely.

For a few happy months, I spent my evenings going round a succession of eighteenth birthday parties in Harrow. Clearly my reputation had spread, and any boy, seeing what his friend had enjoyed on his birthday, would start saving his pocket money months in advance so he could enjoy the same. I'm afraid I teased them dreadfully: nice, well brought up boys all of them, sitting round in a circle enjoying my charms, most of them with cushions on their laps. I revelled in my power, and went as far as I dared with them – might, indeed, have gone a lot further had I not had other appointments waiting, past those boys' bedtimes.

The appointments I most dreaded were those Michelle referred to as 'revenge gigs', where I was roped in to humiliate some poor chap who had doubtless played some practical joke the month before. Usually these gigs went to the Roley-Poley girl, (or 'Grot-a-gram', as she was charmingly advertised): it takes more balls than I'll ever have to sell views of your naked self as a form of punishment, to take your clothes off and expect to elicit laughter. She was a good-natured, single mother in her forties, and took good care to laugh along with the rest, loudest of all: but she hated the job and spoke very bitterly of the men who paid her. Small wonder. She gave up in the end when an unusually large, vicious and determined stag party actually managed to turn her car upside down while she was getting naked, so when she came out she found it spinning plaintively, on its roof, wheels in the air. Poor girl, with her kids waiting at home for her, and no way to get back to them! She screamed, and cried, and made such a noisy fuss that she amassed a small crowd, who managed to right the car and get her home. But the car was never again the same, and neither was she. She got a job in Asda soon after.

Once, I was called to a seventeenth birthday at a slaughterhouse. Now I'm the most squeamish of vegetarians, and I desperately didn't want to do it, but the money was terrific, and Michelle insisted. I got through security, and was dressed as a health and safety inspector: hair back in a blue net, long white coat, thick green wellies. Everything in me was screaming that I should run away. I could smell blood and death in the air. I resolved to make the gig as quick as humanly possible.
Thank God, I was led into a small, but decent office – the wellies had made me worried that I might be cavorting in a puddle of entrails. My relief was short-lived, however, as I saw a young boy being pulled towards me by half a dozen lairy, yelling types, all of them covered in blood. It got worse. As the boy got closer, I saw that he had Down's Syndrome. He wasn't entering into the joke at all. He looked terrified and tearful.
I considered jumping out of the window, but it was too sodding high, and I'm no hero. His mates had us both surrounded, and were snarling at me to get on with it. I made the boy sit down, and gave him the tenderest lap dance I could, keeping eye contact, trying to calm him down. I ignored my usual bag of tricks, and just squirmed as erotically as I could, whilst doing my best to ignore the pool of blood and guts on his lap. I took off my white coat, and remembered I was wearing my favourite white lace underwear. Arse. I decided to take off his white coat too. He didn't seem to mind. In fact, he seemed impervious to everything, even his mates cat calls and taunts, in the face of my pretty, bouncing tits. We had quite a nice time together, and ignored the sadists baying around us. He wanted to shake my hand at the end, but I kissed his cheek instead, working on the assumption he probably hadn't used his cheek to murder any animals. A subdued supervisor handed me the cash and took me back through security. He hadn't had the morning's entertainment, chaos and screaming, he had clearly expected. You'd have thought he'd get enough of that in his daily work, without needing to pay for extra.
At the other extreme, I was asked to a scarily posh part of Hertfordshire to do a full nude strip at a private house - well, 'mansion' would probably be a more appropriate word – at a luncheon party, on Easter Sunday. I wish I could give you an explanation of this, but I have none. I can only guess that one of the guests was making some sort of political statement, or perhaps I was part of a sociological experiment. Half a dozen couples sat round a huge oak table, laden with Port and

Petitsfour, the sun streaming in through the window, Songs of Praise howling out of the telly, and me skipping about showing them all my arse. The women tutted, the men turned puce. And when I'd finished the hostess pressed £70 into my hand and said, with a frosty smile, 'That was quite disgusting.' Well, duh! And you paid for it, you dozy mare.

Occasionally I doubled up with the Grot-a-gram or a male stripper, for anniversary parties and the like, (and *what* an education that was ! The girls would pull and scratch at him until he feared for his sanity: Girls are a perfect nuisance - no sense of propriety), but mainly I worked alone. It made for an odd existence, driving through the night, hundreds of miles, finding lay-bys where I could exchange my school girl outfit for a blonde wig and latex catsuit, then stumbling into oases of bright drunkenness, putting on my happy face for five minutes, before staggering away to do it all over again. I'd arrive home exhausted, sweaty, stinking of sour whipped cream – the bloody stench would get everywhere, and the police hat I kept as a souvenir still stinks of it – and resolve never to do it again. But my purse would bulge thickly with notes, and I found I hadn't the will-power to say no to Michelle's treacly 'Now, Clara, I've got a nice local one for you, a 63 year old gentleman's stag do, nice quiet country pub … ' and having accepted one, felt it incumbent on me to take some of the grottier bookings too.
Often I would end up taking my Gran with me, for company and help with map-reading. Quite often she'd get herself invited into the pub or house, start drinking, and I'd never get her out again. When I had a boyfriend, I'd invite him along instead, finding most men enjoyed feeling protective and proprietorial about their women, barking 'No touching!' if a punter got too close. Usually they enjoyed plotting out the routes too, leaving me free to worry about outfits, make-up and the finer details of the scenarios. ('Silver Peugeot 307, parked illegally!' I'd be muttering, as I ran into the pub; or 'Anne says you're still a naughty boy, and this one's from her …') It seemed I'd never get chance to give the life up, Michelle being in her fifties, and still insanely popular. But then, rather unexpectedly, I found I was pregnant. That tore it.
~~~~~

The next phase
Not a punter, in the end; not anyone at all related to the sex industry, in fact, but a handsome, blonde, corn-fed Canadian I'd met at a party, a friend of a friend of a friend. He thought me very glamorous, with my wicked sex worker ways, little suspecting I was domestic as a kitten. We were together for six months, before I developed a passion for satsumas dunked in marmite. He didn't hang around.
Now I had to make serious money, and my body was no longer my own, but inhabited by a huge, squirming monster. I stripped until I was fourteen weeks gone, took every job going, until my Quality Street tin was bulging with readies. But when the punters' first question was no longer, 'How much for a fuck ?', but 'When are you due?' I thought it was probably time to change course.
I tried to get a proper job for a bit. For now was clearly the perfect time to change career path, four months pregnant and six years of solid sex industry experience behind me: I was an appealing prospect to any employer. I did actually find work,

cleaning a huge industrial estate overnight, 8 p.m. till 5 a.m. It was grim, heavy, lonely work. And then – I don't quite remember how it happened: was it an advertisement from the back of a magazine? – I thought I might try my luck working on a sex-line. The pay wasn't much better, but at least I'd be at home watching my belly swell, rather than lugging it and me round acres of factory floor night after night. And I could work until I went into labour. Hell – probably while I was in labour.

"Aren't you worried its first words will be 'soapy tit wank'?" Finlaye enquired when I told her, always one to get straight to the heart of an issue. I thought I would stop long before baby started talking, preferably a few weeks after birth. I expected to be slipping back into my police outfit and whizzing round the South East's finest hostelries. I was very careful not to put on too much weight. Luckily, my mania for satsumas and marmite stayed with me throughout, and didn't transmogrify into a passion for cheese or lard.

Luckily, too, I didn't suffer much from morning sickness. Many of the requests on 'Cheap Chat', as it was called, were pretty grim. Men wanted to hear me weeing and pooing. A lot. No trouble, I fixed up a jug of water, a tin of beans and a bowl, which did quite nicely. I got myself quite a sound department set up, in fact. The 'great long zip on my leather boots' was actually the fastening of my sleeping bag. The sound of me rubbing my juicy pussy was actually me flapping the inside of my cheek. I would spank a cushion, rather than myself.

The rare morning when I did feel queasy I would always get the class A nutters. The man with the mania for public hangings ('Your cock swells and you ejaculate just before you die. You'd like to see that, wouldn't you?'). The chap who liked to wank with sandpaper, with a skewer down his Jap's eye, his sister's knickers in his mouth … and the chicken. Ah, the chicken. He was one of my first, and soon became a regular. He liked to act out a scenario where I caught him, strangled him, plucked him, basted him and put him in the oven, then went 'Mmmm, mmmm, mmmm! ' as I ate him. He was very sweet. 'Bet you're a vegetarian really, aren't you?' he said once, after I'd smothered him in lemon butter and devoured his thighs and wings. I assured him I wasn't, even as I gagged.

Oh, it was dull! Dull, dull, dull. To make ends meet, I sat by the phone for thirteen hours a day, and most days I took more than three hundred calls, most of them 'one minute wankers', who said very little, and stayed on the line just long enough to get the job done, slamming the phone down at the exact point of orgasm, without even lingering to tell me they still loved and respected me. I got so good at talking them to orgasm, I quickly found I could do it while still reading my book, and would quite resent anyone who broke my concentration to demand something out of the ordinary. My One Minute Script ran something like this :

' Hi, how are you? I'm *horny*. I'm just lying here all alone, nearly naked and juicy wet. I'm dreaming of taking that big thick cock of yours in my mouth – tasting you, teasing you with my tongue - running it up and down the length of your shaft, gently sucking on your balls, one after the other ; then lowering my tight, throbbing wet pussy on to you, riding you, feeling you thrust inside me, over and over, and then crying out in ecstasy as you shoot your *delicious* hot cum...'

That was generally all it took. Over and over I said that. I rigged up a number of phone extensions, so I could make tea, do the ironing, scrub the skirting boards, all while I talked gibberish. It was much trickier when I got a punter who wanted something new and different. My brain ached when I tried to use it, like a limb that's cramped up from lack of use. Given my accent, I seemed to get a lot of men who wanted to be dominated. I had bugger all idea what to do with them. I'd get them to spank themselves, or lick the bottom of a handy shoe, but this didn't seem to work very often, and they didn't come back.

A few men wanted me to pretend to be a man, which puzzled me, as gay chat lines are always so much cheaper. But most of them would end the call by saying they were definitely not gay, despite wanting to call me Richard and imagining my huge cock grazing their tonsils. The human capacity for self-deception remains a wonder to me. I learnt an awful lot about some extraordinary and rare fetishes during those five months. Just when I thought I couldn't be shocked any more, some new pervert would call and knock the wind right out of my sails. Like Denny, who liked to be called a 'filthy nigger' and a 'dirty black bastard' while he masturbated. 'But I'm a Guardian reader!' I kept wailing every minute or so, which only made him wank the harder. There was a funeral director who liked to describe his penchant for corpse-fondling, the necessity of penetrating a corpse before rigor mortis set in, to avoid the orifices 'snapping shut' and trapping the eager member in a rigid and permanent embrace. Sometimes I'd be asked to do a little girl's voice, or listen to how cute the neighbour's six year daughter was, or call the punter 'Daddy' ... I'd hang up on those. There was no way of reporting them, and there were a fair few of them about, though not nearly as many as wanted to hear me have a poo, which I suppose should reassure society somewhat.

At almost nine months pregnant, my phone broke mid-shift, and I was fined for missing more than five calls in one day. Vainly did I protest that it wasn't my fault, that the ringer had broken from overuse, and was it any wonder? Actually, I didn't protest very hard. I was fed up with the whole business. My throat hurt from all the false screams. I never wanted to hear another male voice again. And given that I was about to have a son, I thought I'd better snap out of that pronto.

I spent the last week of my pregnancy sitting my finals, and not saying anything to anyone. It was bliss. I resolved to never, ever get on the phone again to anyone, if I could possibly help it, a resolution I have largely kept.

When my beautiful boy was two weeks old, however, I decided to make an exception: like an idiot, a desperate, greedy idiot, I rang Michelle and claimed my body had snapped back into shape, like magic. It was completely untrue. My belly sagged, I still had my stiches in, and one tit was at least three sizes bigger than the other one. Could I possibly have my old job back? She murmured something non-committal, and I assumed I'd been replaced. It was sickening. There aren't many jobs a single Mum and a new-born can manage, but tearing into a pub, and ripping their clothes off is surely one of them. Arse. My little stash of cash wouldn't last forever. What could I possibly do now ?

Twenty minutes later she rang back.

"Could you do a job this afternoon, do you think?

Oh joy ! ... But then again, 'For Christ's sake!' None of my old clothes fitted me. I had been very careful not to put on excess weight, but still, James had been a huge baby, 10lb 6oz, and the space where he'd been hiding was surely going to sag for a while. I improvised an outfit and shot off to the pub, leaving James behind the bar while I did my turn. It was an eighteenth birthday party. The victim, over-excited and unaccustomed to drink, decided to slip a finger in me once I'd taken my knickers off – me, still with my stitches in! I brought a fist down very sharply on the top of his head; collected my cash and, after a moment's thought, my baby, in dignified silence.

People were always telling me your life changes forever when you have a baby, but I can honestly say that mine didn't, not one bit. I was lucky, no doubt, that James was an easy, amenable child, and I was delighted to devote all my time to him. He'd go to sleep as soon as we got in the car, most of the time, and usually I'd get my Mum or Gran to come with us and sit beside him while I did my thing. Back home, I washed the shaving foam off my tits and feed him, on demand, which soon brought my tummy more or less under control. He slept in my bed at night, and I carried him with me everywhere during the day. At the nicer, family parties, I'd take him inside while I slipped off my outfits, and the women would make a fuss of him while the men ogled the body that made him. So the world turns. At one house, a woman gave me £20 'for the pretty one's money box', and begged to be allowed to touch him, 'for luck' – seemed she'd being trying to have kids of her own for years. I hope it helped.

On one occasion, Michelle asked me to include James in my routine. I'm not proud of agreeing to her suggestion, although remembering it still makes me smile. It was the birthday of a ghastly, tight-arsed bigot, who apparently was often to be heard complaining of 'Bloody immigrants, coming over here, taking our benefits, teaching their kids to beg and steal …' and all that stuff. His chums had come up with the brilliant idea of requesting a stripper with a baby, who would pose as a Kosovan refugee, and go pestering him for money; then, when he loudly and rudely refused, shame him with an incredibly rude, hopefully painful routine. I negotiated a rate for James too of course – no BOGOF deals here – and set about planning. James was very blond to be a Kosovan, so I smeared him in dirt and put a dark hat on him to disguise the worst of his Aryan roots. I put him in a hippy papoose thing I'd borrowed, and wore my shabbiest clothes and boots, topped off with a dark shawl and a few smears of dirt for myself. We did look a disreputable pair! In fact, we got a whole carriage to ourselves on the tube. If you suffer from claustrophobia, I whole-heartedly recommend dressing as an asylum seeker.

The gig went perfectly to plan. It was in quite a posh restaurant, but the manager had been warned to expect me. The only problem was where to put James, once I'd revealed my identity and needed to remove my mucky clothes. One of the bigot's friends looked quite cuddly and paternal, I thought, so I handed James over while I spanked and bullied the birthday boy. James started to whimper hungrily once he saw my tits pop out, and hearing him made me spurt milk all over the bigot's face, which delighted his friends. I was asked to stay for dinner, and we all had a wonderful time in each other's company, even the bigot, and especially James, who was much admired and got all the tit he could handle.

Soon after this I got a follower, who was only too happy to read the maps and babysit while I made the money – we'd first met on the wank-line, and over the course of several evenings we'd devised a code whereby he could find out my phone number. He'd stay every weekend and help. He proved so useful I married him, in time, after several hundred strippergrams. I drove us to Prague for the wedding. He read the map. James carried the rings.

Back home I carried on stripping, but the gigs seemed to be getting rougher. The Grot-a-gram girl got the worst of this, being mouthy and feisty and usually spoiling for a fight. On one job, a girl followed her into the loo and punched her in the face, splitting her lip with a huge sovereign ring. God knows why - she can't have felt jealous or threatened by her. Her entire act consisted of her humiliating herself and sending herself up. Perhaps this girl thought she was so vile and repulsive she needed punishing, or something. Anyway, she drove herself to hospital, one hand on the steering wheel, the other trying to hold together the two pieces of her lip and stem the flow of blood. Ah, why bother trying to understand how these peoples' minds work ?

It was frightening to hear about. But nothing like that ever happened to me. I had a few unpleasant altercations, but nothing I couldn't handle. I'd perfected a posh, charming, dopey persona, all smiles and amiability, so people seemed to feel more inclined to laugh at me than want to hurt me. But I did go to a gig that stopped me, all the same. It was in deepest Essex – not far from the webcam place – a young lad's stag do. The contact met me at the door with the cash.

"Where's your minder, then?"

I got that a lot.

"I don't have one. No need."

"No, you'll be fine. Don't worry."

"I'm not" I said, indifferently, and we walked in. There were about thirty of them, and they encircled me in a tight rugby scrum. They ripped my clothes from me, and took them, and my bag, with car keys, money and phone in, and I was assaulted by seemingly hundreds of fists and fingers. It was extraordinary behaviour. I'd never encountered anything like it. Eventually one of them staggered back, and I fought my way out of the circle, but without clothes or bag I couldn't think what to do next. They were blocking the front door, anyway. I ran out into the pub garden, naked. It was surrounded by a high brick wall with no obvious way out or in, so I tried to climb it, but I fell back, grazing a few bits. A man came over to me, helped me up and put his jacket around me. I didn't know if he was one of the stag party, or a barman, or just another customer: I wasn't taking much in. But he walked me back through the pub, fending off and punching a few of the stag party as they tried to get another grope in. He lent me his phone so I could call the AA and get back into my car, and Michelle, so I could cancel the rest of my work – a piss poor strippergram I would have made, turning up already naked.

Michelle called the police, despite my protestations. They turned up, along with an ambulance, which seemed completely over the top. I showed them the few pathetic marks on my arms and legs, and they tutted, but clearly there wasn't much to see. They recommended I get checked out for STDs, although I doubt there's much you can contract from fingers, however mucky. The police went into the pub and managed to retrieve my bag, although by now it was empty, and a battered police woman's hat. I tossed it onto the back seat, wrapped myself in the foil blanket the ambulance man had left, and drove home.

I was astonished by what had happened to me, and furious too. Later, though, I was scared to death. I couldn't stop revisiting that evening over and over in my head, wondering how I could have handled it better, how I could have acted differently for a happier outcome. But it seemed that whoever had walked into that situation would have met a similar fate. They were spoiling for a fight, that was all. It was nothing personal. Any more than me grinding my snatch against someone's face was anything personal, or covering them in shaving foam and beating them senseless. We were all just doing what we had to do.

But even while I knew that, I also knew I didn't want to do it anymore. I'd been in the sex industry for ten years at this point. Ten years! I didn't have a clue how to do anything else. I had a degree, but much good that would do me with a blank CV and no skills to boast about. I slumped into hopelessness. And I had to go on working, had to. I would get terribly drunk to do it, so I asked my Mum to drive me round, and went into the gigs like an automaton, starting at the least noise or sudden movement. It was no fun for anyone. I started applying for random jobs, lying brazenly on application forms. I still didn't get anywhere. I tried to work at the post office, a care home, a refuge for the victims of domestic abuse. Nothing. Eventually I was offered a job working at a call centre. They didn't care about my history: they were only interested in my charming, dulcet tones, so distinct from the flat estuary English that characterised my neighbours' speech, so useful for flogging insurance. It was a crap job, long hours, tiny salary. I started to realise how extraordinarily lucky I'd been having a job that involved me leaving the house just an evening a week, that still paid all the bills. I missed James terribly, and I was skint. No, this was no way to live! Like a normal person? I think not. All well and good for the people who are born to it, but for me ? ... Never!
I knew, of course, that strippers had a limited shelf life, anyway. I didn't want to become a joke, lugging my tired old tits out of my basque decade after decade. I'd heard the sneers when some of the older girls danced – 'Brought your Grannie along for a day out, have you? Isn't that nice?'– girls who, I now realised, were barely older than me. I wasn't prepared to become a comedy turn, not just yet. What did girls do, in those long, long years between being barely legal and Grot-a-grans ?

I scoured the internet for answers. One line of enquiry particularly attracted me, and recurred in my research more than most. It would suit all of my talents – my fabulous legs, my clipped accent, my imagination, my adventurous nature – and suit my personality too. It was so obvious I couldn't believe it hadn't occurred to me before. I would become a Dominatrix.
~~~~~

Back to the present
A website group down in the South West of England was advertising for models. They had half a dozen websites, largely female to male spanking, a few female to female. I signed up for a day's work, involving a handful of films, some where I'd be receiving, most where I'd be dishing it out. I thought it would make an excellent introduction to my new career. And it meant £200, which by this time I badly bloody needed. I'd spoken to Tara on the phone and she sounded charming.

"Bring all your clothes" she told me. "All of them. We'll have a rummage through and see what's suitable."

The director didn't like to plan ahead, apparently: he received inspiration from the outfits the girls chose to bring, believing this would express their inner personalities.

"He sounds a prick ! " I told her gaily, although as soon as I'd said it I knew she was going to tell me the prick was her boyfriend. She did. She was very nice about it. And when I turned up, he was actually quite good fun. I packed my battered police woman's outfit, a slutty school girl costume, a few glittery stripper dresses, a leather basque, and a couple of smart suits. All he wanted, however, was the manky top and jeans I'd travelled down in, sweating nervously every second.

We did have fun! It was a pretty small, budget operation, with his mate, Gary, doing the camera work, David directing. We spent the first hour taking photos of me being spanked – not hard, just enough to show the impact on my flesh. They kept up a nice steady rhythm so the photographer would know exactly when to take the picture. It was very restful. Then I spanked Tara, although as a pro-sub she had a hide like rhino, and I could barely make a dent on her. When she spanked me, however, the cameraman politely told me that my screaming was making a mockery of his sound levels. There is a knack to taking a spanking. You have to think of the heat as something pleasant, like a tropical sun beating down on your glistening buttocks, on a Caribbean beach. You need to use your breathing, like being in labour. Seeing how I was struggling, even with a hand and paddle, Tara gave me the gentlest of taps with the cane. David complained that it looked faked, and that he needed some stripes. Almost in tears on my behalf – she really is the sweetest of girls – she gave me six corking blows across my backside. How I howled, and danced, and wished I were dead. I couldn't believe anyone would pay for this insanity. But when I placed my first advertisement on the website she recommended, I discovered that finding punters wouldn't be the problem. The problem would be finding enough hours to fit them all in.

The hours, and the location. My new husband refused to let me use our house, reasonably enough, I suppose. I didn't much want to rent a dungeon – expensive, and not exactly the vibe I was aiming to project: I hoped to specialise in domestic discipline, headmistress, auntie, school prefect, gym instructor, strict female boss, that sort of thing, rather than go in for leather basques and bondage, about which I knew precisely nothing. I asked a few friends and neighbours if they fancied a few extra quid, just for popping out and leaving me their house keys – but even the poorest of them seemed reluctant. I struggled to understand why, but I suppose if you haven't been in the sex industry half your life, it could seem quite a big deal to turn your home into a part-time quasi-brothel. And the neighbours, of course : always the worry of the neighbours! Spanking is a noisy bloody business. Even if the man isn't a squealer, the crisp and unmistakeable sound of a cane whistling through the air and landing on an upturned pair of buttocks always seems to carry through walls, however loud you turn up the telly. Desperate, I did what all desperate girls do: I asked my Mum for help. And she agreed I could rent her house, bless her, as and when I needed it. She even agreed to hide in a cupboard if a chap sounded dodgy.

I had very little equipment at the start. I had no idea how much would be needed, or what I wanted to use. I bought a tawse and a cane from the local sex shop, found a couple of slippers, a wooden spoon, a belt and a hairbrush, and decided I was good to go.

My first spankee was an absolute charmer. He was in his early sixties, very experienced and remarkably forgiving. I'd got quite drunk to get me through that initial horror of not knowing what to do or how to behave. I'm not naturally dominant, and telling people to 'stand here', 'bend over', 'take down your trousers and pants' seemed alien and bizarre. He told me exactly what he liked, praised me when I managed it, and forgave all my shortcomings, even the tipsy tripping over in my stilettos. He was great. I still see him occasionally, bless him.

I've been doing it full time for about six years now, but I've never got any better at telling people what to do. I'm still, really, as I quite often have to warn people, a crap dominatrix. I find myself asking the punters all the time if I'm doing it right for them, if I'm hitting them too hard or not enough, if it isn't actually rather uncomfortable to be balanced across a concrete floor, with metal clips on your bollocks. Some men really appreciate my giggly, caring approach to punishment. To those that don't, there are plenty of other girls out there to tell them what to do, and mean it. I'm probably the most submissive dominatrix on the scene. I can do role play, and beat men until they bleed, if that's honestly what they want, but I'm never happier than during the five minute switch at the end, that so many of them request, when I relax over their laps and take a gentle spanking. I can see the appeal: it's very restful being told what to do. Personally, I think the true submissive makes a much better play partner than the dominant type: they understand the appeal of losing control, and they also, more crucially, yearn to please.

About a year after I started, my Mum turned sixty five, and had to retire from her schmuck job with P&O Ferries. Impressed with the money I earned, and the stacks of presents I got – jewels and flowers mainly, but also knickers, stockings, books and gin – she decided to have a go herself. And why not? It's a great job. You choose your own hours and clients. If I ever meet a girl with long legs and a reasonably good vocabulary, I always recommend she turn professional disciplinarian. It's definitely the best job I've ever had. It fulfils every aspect of me, from my exhibitionism to my creativity. I get to write, act, wear glamorous outfits, primp and preen and be worshipped, by men who, at Oxford, would have gone out of their way to spit on me. If you can't join them, beat them!

Recently, I've decided to expand the business into adult baby, foot fetish and enforced feminisation. I'm considering running spanking holidays, and teaching domination classes. There's no end to the ways men want to be challenged and humiliated, it seems. I've started working with other girls, and conquered my fear of dungeons and bondage.

My Mum, now sixty nine, earns more than I do. They do love the older girls! And indeed, the wrinklier I get, the more money I seem to earn. You've no need for a pension plan if you know how to wield a cane. And a Mother and Daughter domination double act is still rare enough to get them queuing round the block. She's better than me at role-play, making them wait, making them anxious. She loves having them squirm at her feet. But my aim is better, frankly, so it all pans out in the long run.

Slowly, over the years, I've built up a client base of absolute charmers, many of whom have become good friends. There's something about a submissive man. They tend to be clever and charming, and really good fun. I could tell you some stories ... but I won't, because this is my life just now, and I don't spank and tell. You'll have to wait until I've moved onto the next big thing before I'll give you any mucky details. Anyway, you can read all about my current adventures on the blog!

I'll leave you with one final anecdote. My third client, 'C', just wanted me to look at 1950's porn with him, while I flicked his nipples. This went on for about forty minutes, him looking at basques and waspies, me flicking, until my nails ached, both of us in perfect silence. Finally he turned to me and said
"For the next session, could I possibly eat your poo ? "
"Um ..."
"Is there a particular time I'd need to turn up? ... It would need to be fresh, obviously ... "
"Well, that goes without saying."
He looked at me for a moment, then beamed understandingly.
"And of course, I'd bring my own knife and fork."